201
QUILT BLOCKS

201
QUILT BLOCKS

Motifs, projects, and ideas

Louise Bell

CICO BOOKS

LONDON NEW YORK

Published in 2008 by CICO Books
an imprint of Ryland Peters & Small
519 Broadway, 5th Floor,
New York, NY 10012

www.cicobooks.co.uk

10 9 8 7 6 5 4 3 2 1

A CIP catalog record for this book is
available from the Library of Congress

ISBN-13: 978 1 906094 95 9

Printed in China

Editors: Sarah Hoggett, Marion Paull
Designer: Ian Midson
Photographer: Geoff Dann
Illustrator: Stephen Dew

Contents

Introduction

Becoming a quilt maker was an accident just waiting to happen. I made a patchwork quilt as I waited for my University results, thudding the patches together on an old manual sewing machine and then quilting by hand. It was an awful lot of sewing. A neighbor asked if I would make another to sell in her craft shop: What else did I make? Well, I decided I would make anything she asked for—just as soon as I could get my hands on an electric sewing machine.

I had never thought of quilt making as a job—careers advisors had not suggested it and I had never met any craftspeople who earned a living through their work. I did, however, know people (most of my family, in fact) who were passionate about making things, building things, and drawing or painting things, and I spent most of my spare time doing the same. As I seemed to have an irresistible urge to create, doing it for a living seemed not only to be my perfect occupation, but something of a privilege.

The Pineapple block (see page 116) is Log Cabin with a twist. For this pattern strips are pieced diagonally, as well as horizontally and vertically.

My first quilt, Grandmother's Fan, was the same design as a quilt we had at home. My Canadian great grandmother had made it as a wedding gift for my parents. As a child, I had spent hours looking at the fabrics, tracing the design with my finger, counting the colors and patches, trying to make sense of this busy, lively pattern. When I later compared mine with hers, I realized I had not remembered it quite right. I had made an impression of the quilt, based on hazy

memories. There are hundreds of traditional American block designs, and I suspect that some of this proliferation is due to faulty memories like mine. As I looked at other quilts and learnt how to draft blocks, I discovered how knowing just a few simple rules could help jog my memory and make sense of a puzzling quilt. Four-patch is a block divided in four, while seven-patch has seven patches; draw a square and divide it up to make your templates. Simple. Rotate some of the patches or subdivide them to produce new patterns then alter color placements and scale to change the effect yet again. One of the hardest things to achieve is an exact copy of someone else's quilt, and that's the best part of it: whatever you make will be unique and personal to you.

Most of the other quilts we had at home were traditional geometric block designs. Some of the best ones had fabric repeats while some, the everyday ones, seemed more and more confusing the closer I looked. From a distance, the design appeared

Gentleman's Fancy (see page 34) looks at first glance like the foundation block Snail Trail, with its central square and triangles pieced around the middle. It is, in fact, a nine-patch block. To draft accurate templates, you must divide the grid into nine rather than four.

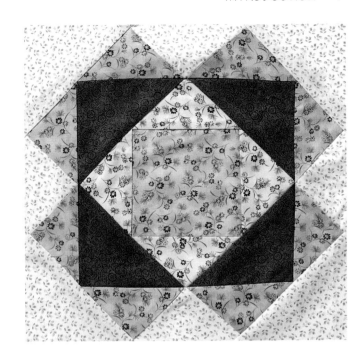

clear, but close up the patches seemed random, and some of the smallest patches were themselves patched. These scrap quilts were a way of making something useful and beautiful out of not very much at all—the main ingredients being the quilter's need for economy combined with a desire to make sense and order from a scrap bag. When you start making quilts you discover that those little bags of irresistible fabrics soon become stacks. They fill shelves, sometimes whole rooms, and the box of leftovers grows and grows. Quilts like the Nine Patch framed

in printed lawns (see page 118) and the Bird and tulip ring (page 150) are ideal for keeping the fabric stash tamed, while the Child's counting quilt (page 130) and Tumbling Blocks (page 122) are the perfect way to use favourite leftovers and memory snippets.

I enjoy using highly patterned lawns that blur and soften geometric shapes. I also love plain fabrics—rich and vibrant silks that shout the block designs. And then there are the appliqué designs. Doves, hearts, and tulips feature on many vintage quilts, their simple shapes are so easily recognizable. But iris and bluebell, roosters and hens, seahorses and shells can all be just as striking.

When working to commission I take notes of the likes and dislikes of my customers and try to make an impression of the quilt they will enjoy. I like working out how to appliqué favorite plants—thistles and

Grandmother's Fan (see page 124) is traditionally pieced with blocks edge to edge, or with alternating plain squares between each one. The project quilt has sashing strips and the blocks have been rotated to give a central flower design.

dandelions will push me a bit harder as the plants don't naturally lend themselves to the stylized shapes of appliqué.

I love pattern, shape, and colors that blend and can rarely resist filling my work up with all three elements. Inspiration comes from anywhere and everywhere—the second quilt I made was, I thought, entirely original, until I looked down and saw a similar pattern on a Victorian tiled floor. I once put some pea pod shapes in a quilt. A while later I opened a book I had read some time before and there it was, a tiny design at the start of every chapter. I would like to acknowledge everyone whose ideas and designs have inspired me, but I am rarely aware of where the ideas come from. Patterns, motifs, and arrangements seem to seek me out, hiding in my subconscious until the perfect project comes along.

Monogrammed pillows (see page 140) make the perfect gift for a loved one and are straightforward to make. Use the alphabet templates on page 90 to personalize your block.

I had spent hours and weeks making my first quilt and an electric machine was essential when I decided to turn play into work. Quilt making is my job—so what of my spare time? I stitch by hand. I think up ever more complex appliqué designs for beds and walls. I sew and make quilts, taking as long as I want, because I just like doing it.

I hope this book will inspire you to start that quilt, make that memory pillow, use up that tantalizing fabric you've been saving, try out something new, or adapt a design to suit your taste.

Louise Bell

Bird and leaf ring pillow (see page 143). As an alternative, try using the Butterfly or Dragonfly motifs (see page 65).

PATCHWORK BLOCKS

To draft blocks accurately, draw a square the size you want the stitched block to be and divide it into patches—four, five, seven, nine, or even hexagon and star shapes. Next, subdivide the patches to make the individual block design. The sizes given are suggestions—you can create larger or smaller finished pieces simply by redrafting the block.

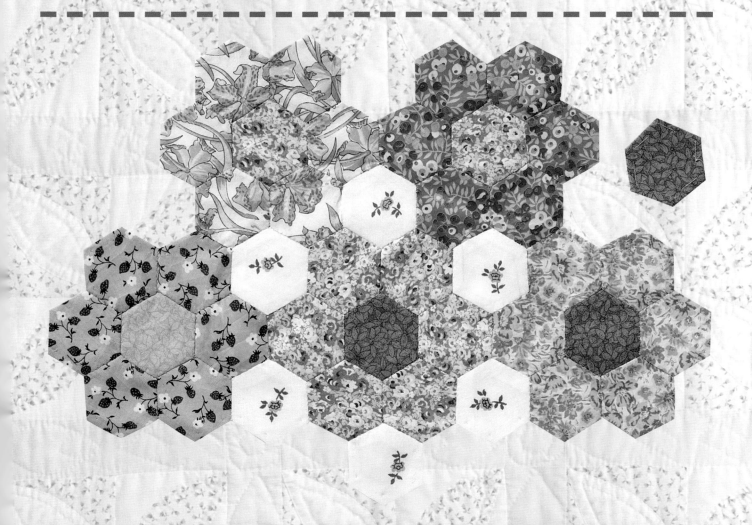

Four-patch blocks

Patchwork blocks that have two equal sections across the top, or a multiple of two sections, are called four-patch blocks. Some blocks, such as Fly, have four patches that are identical and are rotated to form the design. Others, such as Broken Dishes, have identical design patches in two color variations. Ann and Andy has two different design patches, while in Flower Basket each quarter is different.

Four Patch

Size of finished block: 6 in. square

Size of each finished patch: 3 in. square

When it is pieced in two colors only, Four Patch looks like a checkerboard. Using three colors and piecing them uniformly together with the same color top right and bottom left each time creates a diagonal chain effect, while using a different color for each patch gives the block a jewel-like effect.

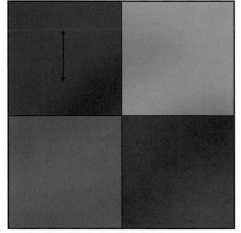

One patch, four colors

■ Draft the template (see page 160) and cut four squares in two, three, or four colors.

■ First, piece the upper and lower patches together to form two vertical strips, and press the seams in opposite directions.

■ Pin the two strips together, carefully aligning the seams, and stitch slowly to prevent the patches from slipping out of position. Press the vertical seam; it does not matter which way you press it, but for a whole quilt, press all the vertical seams the same way.

Broken Dishes

Size of finished block: 6 in. square

Size of each finished patch: 3 in. square

In two contrasting colors, this design looks dramatic, like ceramic tiles, and using four contrasting colors (as here) creates a chain effect when rotated across the quilt.

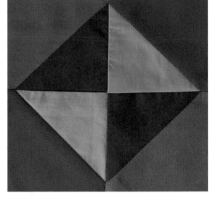

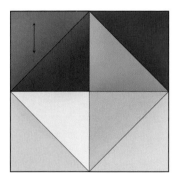

One patch, rotated repeat

■ Draft the template (see page 160) and cut two triangles each in red, blue, pale green, and dark green. The fabric grain on all pieces must run either vertically or horizontally.

■ Piece the triangle squares—red/pale green, blue/dark green—and press the seams toward the darker fabric.

■ Lay the patches out in sequence and piece as for Four Patch, pinning before stitching to ensure that the seams align and the points meet at the center.

Windmill

Size of finished block: 6 in. square

Size of each finished patch: 3 in. square

Windmill has diagonally quartered patches, with the grain line running in a different direction on the large and small triangles. Paler outer triangles increase the pinwheel effect.

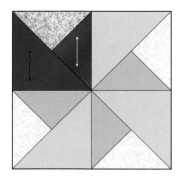

One patch, rotated repeat

■ Draft the templates (see page 160) and cut four large triangles in red and four small triangles each in green and a sprigged white.

■ Assemble the small triangles first. Lay pale on dark and machine stitch along one short side to make four identical large triangles. Press the seams toward the darker fabric.

■ Sew these triangles to the red triangles along the long edge to make triangle squares, then press the seams toward the large triangles.

■ Lay the patches out in sequence and piece as for Four Patch, pinning before stitching to ensure that the seams align and the points meet at the center.

Fly

Size of finished block: 6 in. square

Size of each finished patch: 3 in. square

If this block is worked in just two colors and the blocks are joined without sashing, the effect will be the same as two-tone Broken Dishes. The design works best with alternating blocks in two colorways.

■ Draft the template (see page 160) and cut four triangles in each of two colors. The fabric grain on all pieces must run either vertically or horizontally, otherwise the block will stretch out of shape; always mark the direction of grain on the templates.

■ Piece the triangle squares and press the seams toward the darker fabric.

■ Lay the patches out in sequence and piece as for Four Patch, pinning before stitching to ensure that the seams align and the points meet at the center.

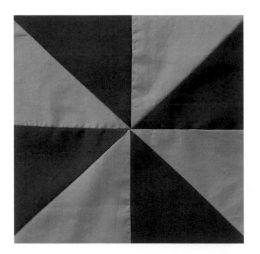

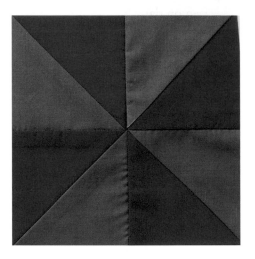

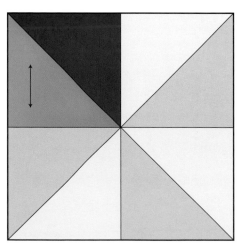

One patch, rotated repeat

Fly in two colorways, alternating blocks

Big Dipper

Size of finished block: 6 in. square

Size of each finished patch: 3 in. square

For the most dramatic effect, use contrasting tones on the inner and outer triangles.

■ Draft the template (see page 160) and cut four triangles in each of four contrasting colors, with the grain line running along the long edge of each triangle.

■ Lay pale green on dark green and blue on red, and stitch along one short side to make four identical large triangles in each colorway. Press the seams towards the darker fabric.

■ Lay out the triangles in sequence and piece them into triangle squares, being careful to match up the seams at the centers. Press the seams in alternate directions.

■ Continue as for Four Patch, pinning before stitching to ensure that the seams align and the points meet at the center.

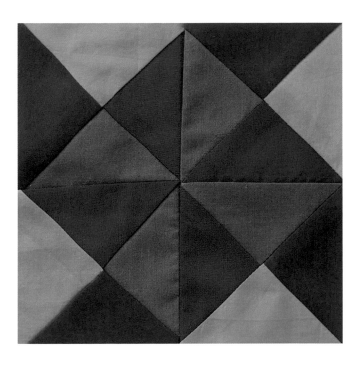

BIG DIPPER BLOCKS SET EDGE TO EDGE

If Big Dipper blocks are set edge to edge, they resemble Fly in two colorways (see facing page) but with a diagonal set.

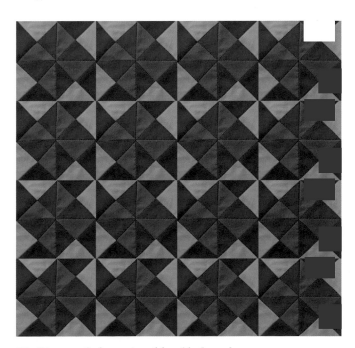

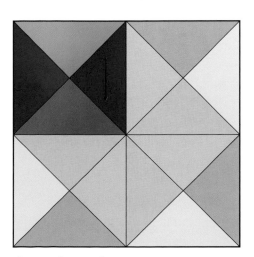

One patch, rotated repeat

Big Dipper quilt, four strips of four blocks each

FOUR-PATCH BLOCKS OF MULTIPLE PATCHES

The four-patch blocks on pages 14–20 each have four patches across and four patches down, and the last four-patch block on page 21 has eight patches across and eight patches down. Most of the blocks are first pieced into patches, then into vertical strips. The individual patches—squares or triangle squares—are assembled in different sequences to make a variety of blocks. You can restrict yourself to just two colors per block or choose up to five to change the look of each block even more.

Ann and Andy

Size of finished block: 12 in. square

Size of each finished patch: 3 in. square

In this design, the top left and lower right quarters are all made up of triangle squares, while the top right and lower left quarters are a combination of triangle squares and squares. If blocks are placed edge to edge on a quilt top, without blank squares or sashing in between, the diagonal string of squares takes prominence and gives a diagonal chain effect across a quilt. In a strong or bright shade, this can look really striking.

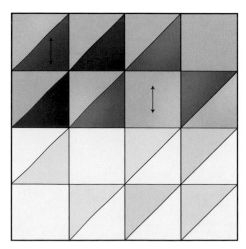

Two quarter blocks, mirrored

■ Draft the templates (see page 160) and cut four pale squares and 12 matching pale triangles. Cut six triangles in one dark shade, four in another, and two in a third.

■ Piece the 12 triangle squares (pale/dark) and press the seams toward the darker color.

■ Lay the patches out in sequence, piece into four vertical strips, and press the seams in alternate directions. Sew the strips together and press all the vertical seams in the same direction across the block.

Triangle Squares

Size of finished block: 12 in. square

Size of each finished patch: 3 in. square

This is a repeating patch block, so you only need to draft one quarter; however, there are two different color sequences and the quarters are rotated through 90° to create the pattern. The design works best with triangles in strongly contrasting tones.

■ Draft the templates (see page 160) and cut two squares each in navy and mauve. Cut 12 triangles in yellow, and six each in blue and green.

■ Piece the triangle squares (yellow/green, yellow/blue) and press the seams toward the darker fabrics.

■ Lay the patches out in sequence and piece into four vertical strips, pinning near the seams to keep the points aligned. Press the seams in opposite directions. Sew the strips together and press all the vertical seams in the same direction across the block.

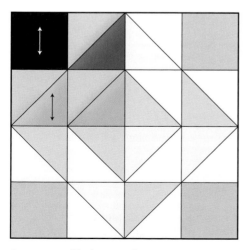

One quarter block, rotated repeat

TRIANGLE SQUARES BLOCKS SET EDGE TO EDGE
If the blocks are assembled without sashing, alternating the color of the corner squares adds interest as little Four Patch blocks appear between the diamonds. Here, nine Triangle Squares blocks have been pieced together in three strips of three.

Double X

Size of finished block: 12 in. square

Size of each finished patch: 3 in. square

This block works well when the center squares are in a different tone or color than the outer squares and triangle squares, as the Four Patch center stands out.

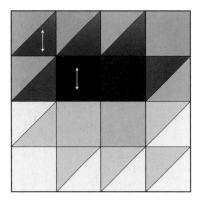

Two quarter blocks, mirrored

■ Draft the templates (see page 160) and cut two squares each in lilac, purple, and navy, and ten triangles each in lilac and mauve.

■ Piece the triangle squares (pale/dark) and press the seams toward the darker color.

■ Lay the patches out in sequence. Pin near the seams to keep the points aligned, piece into four vertical strips, and press the seams in alternate directions. Sew the strips together and press all the vertical seams in the same direction across the block.

Indian Star

Size of finished block: 12 in. square

Size of each finished patch: 3 in. square

This is a repeating patch block, but it has two different sets of color—so it is important to lay the block out before you piece it in order to get the color sequence right.

■ Draft the templates (see page 160) and cut two squares each in lilac, yellow, green, and blue and eight triangles each in navy and pale green.

■ Piece the triangle squares (navy/pale green) and press the seams toward the darker color.

■ Lay the patches out in sequence. Piece into vertical strips, pinning near the seams to keep the points aligned, and press the seams in alternate directions. Sew the strips together and press all the vertical seams in the same direction across the block.

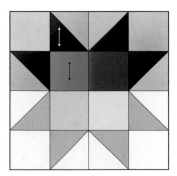

One quarter block, rotated repeat

Diamond Star and Crystal Star

Size of finished block: 12 in. square

Size of each finished patch: 3 in. square

The only difference between these blocks is the positioning of the central triangle squares. Both are repeating patch blocks in which the patch is rotated to create the pattern, with alternating colors on the corners.

■ For either block, draft the templates (see page 160) and cut two mid-mauve and two green squares, eight navy and eight pale green triangles, and four triangles each in dark mauve and yellow for the centers.

■ Piece the triangle squares (navy/pale green and yellow/dark mauve) and press the seams toward the darker fabric.

■ Lay the patches out in sequence. Piece into four vertical strips, pinning near the seams to keep the points aligned, and press the seams in alternate directions. Sew the strips together and press all the vertical seams in the same direction across the block.

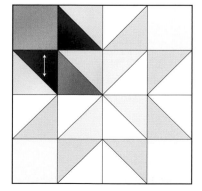

DIAMOND STAR

One quarter block, rotated repeat

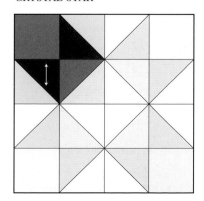

CRYSTAL STAR

One quarter block, rotated repeat

Chevron

Size of finished block: 12 in. square

Size of each finished patch: 3 in. wide

Chevron can be confusing to assemble as the patches repeat left to right, with different colors top and bottom.

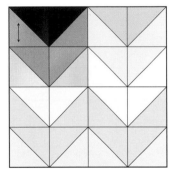

One quarter block, straight repeat

■ Draft the template (see page 160) and cut eight triangles each in lilac, yellow, and mauve, and four each in green and dark mauve.

■ Lay the pieces out in sequence. Piece into triangle squares and press the seams toward the darker fabric.

■ Lay the patches out in sequence. Piece into four vertical strips, pinning near the seams to keep the points aligned. Press the seams in alternate directions. Sew the strips together and press all vertical seams in the same direction across the block.

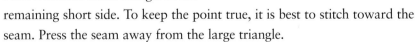

Flying Geese

Size of finished block: 12 in. square

Size of each finished patch: 3 in. wide

Using a pale tone for the small triangles on the right-hand side of each quarter and a mid-tone on the left creates a pin-wheel effect.

■ Draft the templates (see page 160) and cut four large triangles in navy and four in purple, and 16 small triangles in yellow. The grain direction is very important, so make sure you mark it on the templates.

■ Piece the long side of a small triangle to the short side of a large triangle. Press the seam away from the large triangle. Piece a second small triangle to the remaining short side. To keep the point true, it is best to stitch toward the seam. Press the seam away from the large triangle.

■ Piece two triangle rectangles together to form a quarter of the block, with a purple/yellow rectangle at the top of the quarter and a navy/yellow rectangle at the base. Press the seam toward the purple. Make another identical quarter block and then make two more quarters, reversing the colors so that purple/yellow rectangles are at the base.

■ Arrange the patches and piece as for Four Patch (see page 10).

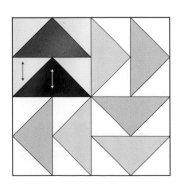

One quarter block, rotated repeat

Batchelor's Puzzle

Size of finished block: 12 in. square

Size of each finished patch: 3 in. square

To achieve the effect of rectangular boxes, use the darkest tone for the squares, the lightest for the center and corner triangles, and a mid-tone for the other triangles.

■ Draft the templates (see page 160) and cut four blue squares and eight triangles each in yellow, green, and purple.

■ Piece the triangle squares (four yellow/green, four yellow/purple, four purple/green) and press the seams toward the darker fabric.

■ Lay the patches out in sequence; even though the quarters are identical, this is a confusing block to assemble. Piece into four vertical strips, and press the seams in alternate directions. Sew the strips together and press all the vertical seams in the same direction across the block.

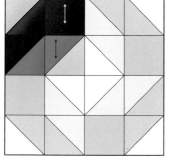

One quarter block, rotated repeat

Mosaic

Size of finished block: 12 in. square

Size of each finished patch: 3 in. square

This block works best pieced edge to edge, without sashing or alternating plain squares. The red-based designs will stand out when repeated across a quilt. Alternating the colors on the outer triangles will give even more interest.

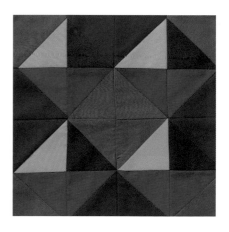

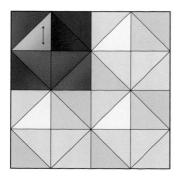

One quarter block, straight repeat

■ Draft the template (see page 160) and cut eight triangles each in red, blue, and dark green, and four each in pale green and purple.

■ Piece the triangle squares—four blue/red, two blue/pale green, two blue/purple, four dark green/red, two dark green/pale green, and two dark green/purple.

■ Lay the patches out in sequence. Piece the four vertical strips and press the seams in alternate directions. Sew the strips together and press all the vertical seams in the same direction across the block.

Old Maid's Puzzle

Size of finished block: 12 in. square

Size of each finished patch: 3 in. square

This block has two different quarters to draft—top left (repeated lower right) and top right (repeated lower left). All the triangles have the grain line running along a short edge.

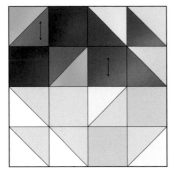

Two quarter blocks, mirrored

■ Draft the templates (see page 160) and cut two red squares and six red triangles, four navy squares, six yellow triangles, four green triangles, and four blue triangles.

■ Piece the triangle squares (red/yellow and blue/green) and press the seams toward the darker fabrics.

■ Lay the patches out in sequence. Piece into four vertical strips and press the seams in alternate directions. Sew the strips together and press all the vertical seams in the same direction across the block.

Flower Basket

Size of finished block: 12 in. square

Size of each finished patch: 3 in. square

This design works best with sashing or alternating plain squares, so that the stylized basket is not lost.

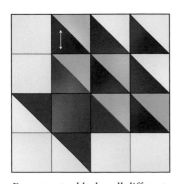

■ Draft the templates (see page 160) and cut one red square and four red triangles, five yellow squares and five yellow triangles, five green triangles, three navy triangles, two purple triangles, and one mid-blue triangle.

■ Piece the triangle squares (two yellow/red, two yellow/purple, one yellow/ mid blue, three green/navy, and two green/red). Press the seams toward the darker fabrics.

■ Lay the patches out in sequence before piecing. Pin near the seams to keep all the seams aligned and piece into four vertical strips.

■ Press the seams in alternate directions. Sew the strips together, again pinning carefully, and press all the vertical seams in the same direction across the block.

Four quarter blocks, all different

Odd Fellow's Chain

Size of finished block: 24 in. square

Size of finished quarter block: 12 in. square

Size of each finished patch: 3 in. square

Odd Fellow's Chain is a four-patch block, but it has eight patches across and down, making 64 squares or triangle squares to piece. A nonslip board is essential for laying out the pieces before assembling. It is best not to attempt to make this block too small. I made this one twice the size of the others, in order to place it in the center of the Four-patch Sampler Quilt (page 117).

Although it is hard to make out, you'll see that each quarter of this block is a Double X (see page 16) and an Indian Star (see page 16) has appeared in the center.

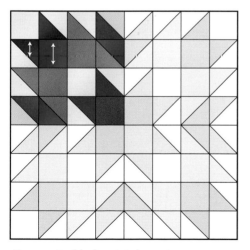

One quarter block, rotated repeat

■ Draft the templates (see page 160) and cut eight squares and 24 triangles in yellow, eight squares and 16 triangles in mid-blue, two squares and eight triangles in navy, four squares and eight triangles in dark green, two squares in purple, 16 triangles in red, and eight triangles in pale green.

■ Make sure that the grain line (running along a short side) is maintained on all the triangles and cut the pieces very accurately.

■ Piece all the triangle squares—eight green/mid blue, eight red/pale green, and all the others pieced to a yellow. Press the seams toward the darker fabrics and lay the patches out in sequence on a design board.

■ Piece vertical strips of eight patches. Press all the seams of each strip in alternating directions across the block. Sew the strips together and press all the vertical seams in the same direction.

Five-patch blocks

Five-patch blocks are more difficult to draft and piece than four- and nine-patch blocks, since they are not always put together in strips of equal width. The diagrams show the easiest ways to assemble them. Some blocks with borders show how they would look with sashing.

Lady of the Lake

Size of finished block: 12½ in.
Size of each finished small triangle-square patch:
2½ in.

This block is assembled diagonally. One half is made up of triangle squares around two edges of a triangle, while the other is a large plain triangle. The block works best without sashing or alternating plain squares, and in contrasting colors.

■ Draft the templates (see page 160) and cut seven small dark triangles and nine small pale triangles, one medium pale triangle, and one large triangle in dark fabric. The grain lines must run along the short side of all triangles.

■ Piece seven dark/pale triangle squares and press the seams toward the darker fabric. If the fabric has a pattern direction it should be constant across the block, so make sure you assemble each one the same way (lay dark fabric over pale and always stitch on the same side).

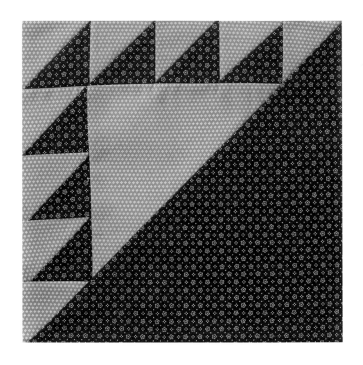

■ Sew together three triangle squares with an extra pale triangle at the bottom, and press the seams towards the darker fabric.

■ Sew together four triangle squares with an extra pale triangle on the right and press the seams toward the darker fabric.

■ Sew the first triangle squares strip to one short edge of the medium-sized pale triangle, so that all the pale triangles point the same way, and press the seam toward the large triangle.

■ Sew the second triangle squares strip to the remaining short edge of the medium triangle, and press the seam away from the small triangles.

■ Sew this triangle to the large dark triangle.

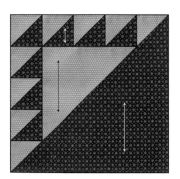

Triangle squares, straight repeat

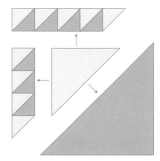

left-hand strip = 1, top strip = 2, small triangle = 3.

Grape Basket

Size of finished block without border: 12½ in.

Size of each finished triangle-square patch: 2½ in.

This block works best alternating with plain squares on a quilt or as a single block with a border around, so the stylized basket shape is not lost.

■ Draft the templates (see page 160) and cut 13 small triangles and eight squares in gray, six small tan triangles, five small mid-green floral triangles, two small dark green triangles, and one large triangle each in gray and dark green.

■ Piece the small triangle squares—six gray/tan, five gray/mid-green, and two gray/dark green—and one large gray/dark green triangle square.

■ Lay the patches out in sequence; note that the triangle squares do not follow the same direction. Piece vertical strips 1, 2, and 5 and press the seams in alternate directions.

■ For strips 3 and 4, piece the tan/gray, green/gray, and dark green/gray triangle squares into horizontal pairs and then assemble the wide vertical strip, pressing the horizontal seams in a different direction from the seams in strips 2 and 5.

■ Sew these four strips together.

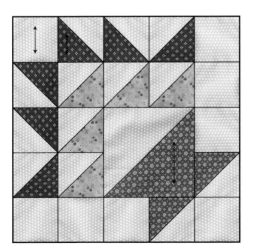

Triangle squares, rotated repeat

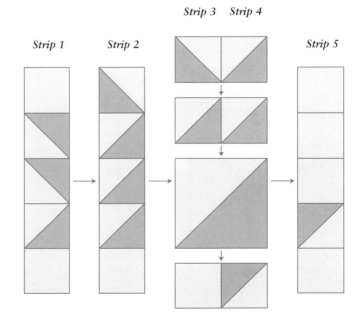

Strip 1   Strip 2   Strip 3   Strip 4   Strip 5

Goose Tracks

Size of finished block without border: 12½ in.

Size of each finished small three-triangle patch: 2½ in.

The block is shown with a border. Omitting the border and placing the blocks side by side changes Goose Tracks' appearance dramatically.

■ Draft the templates (see page 160) and cut eight tiny triangles each in cream and green, eight larger triangles in tan, four squares each in cream and tan, one green square for the center, and four rectangles in bright green. The fabric grain runs along the long edge of the tiny triangles and along the short edges of the larger triangles.

■ First, piece the tiny triangles to make larger triangles. The pairs are mirror images, so place half the green triangles on cream and half the cream triangles on green and stitch along the right-hand short side. Press the seams toward the darker fabric.

■ Sew the cream and green triangles to the tan triangles to make eight triangle squares, and press the seams toward the tan fabric.

■ Lay out in sequence and piece four identical patches: cream square above triangle square and mirror image triangle square above tan square. Piece upper to lower patch, then piece left side to right side. Pin either side of the cross seam so that the seams and points in the center align, and stitch slowly.

■ Lay these pieced squares out in sequence along with the remaining patches and piece into three vertical strips. Press the seams in alternate directions and sew the strips together.

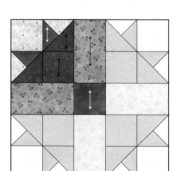

One corner section, rotated around center square and strip

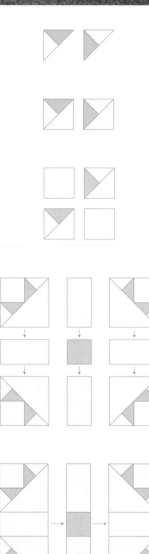

Pin Wheel

Size of finished block without border: 12½ in.

Size of each finished corner-square patch: 2½ in.

Pin Wheel has triangles with different grain directions, plus some acute angles to match up, but only one design patch, which is rotated around a central square.

■ Draft the templates (see page 160) and cut four tall triangles each in cream and red, four squares in red, four tiny triangles each in mid green and cream, four larger triangles each in spotted and dark green, and one dark green square.

■ Piece the tall (red/cream) triangle rectangles and press the seams toward the darker color.

■ Piece the large triangles (dark green/spotted) along a short edge to form larger triangles, laying the pale fabric over the dark and stitching down the right-hand edge each time so that the patches are identical. Press the seams toward the darker color.

■ Place a tiny cream triangle on a red square and sew the short edge of the triangle to the right-hand edge of the square. Press the seam away from the square. Piece a mid-green triangle to the top edge of the red. Make three more of these new triangles. Press the seams toward the darker fabric.

■ Lay the pieces out in sequence and make the four corner triangle squares, pinning near the cross seams to align the seams and ensure that the points meet in the center.

■ Assemble into three vertical strips, pressing the seams in alternate directions strip by strip, and finally sew the strips together.

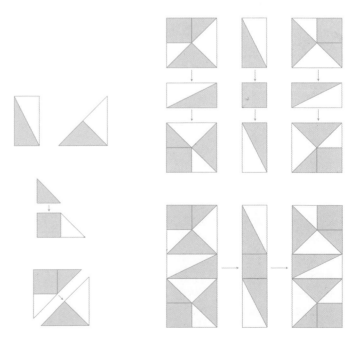

One corner section, rotated repeat

Double Irish Chain

Size of finished block: 12½ in.

Size of each finished small square patch: 2½ in.

This is a two-block design. It is best to use either a patterned pale fabric or one that is fairly opaque; otherwise, you will have to trim dark fabrics at the seams to prevent them from showing through. You need at least nine blocks in total to see the chain effect.

BLOCK A

■ Draft the template (see page 160) and cut 12 red, nine mid-green, and four pale squares.

■ Lay the squares out in sequence and piece into five vertical strips. Press each seam toward the darker fabric.

■ Sew the strips together and press all the vertical seams in the same direction.

BLOCK B

■ Draft the templates (see page 160) and cut four small red squares, four rectangles, and one large central square in the pale fabric.

■ Sew a rectangle to each side of the central square. Sew a red square to each end of the remaining rectangles and sew these to the top and lower edges of the square. Press the seams toward the darker fabric.

BLOCK A

BLOCK B

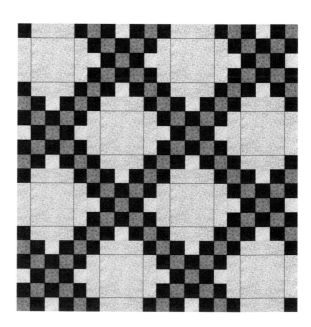

Block A

Block B

Flying Birds

Size of finished block without border: 12½ in.

Size of each finished patch: 2½ in.

The block is shown with a dark border to show how it would look assembled on a quilt with sashing or with alternating plain blocks. Placing the blocks side by side changes the appearance dramatically, as hexagonal shapes with intersecting squares appear.

■ Draft the templates (see page 160) and cut eight tan triangles and four tan squares, eight gray triangles and eight gray squares, four mid-green squares, and one dark green square.

■ Piece the tan/gray triangle squares; if the fabrics have a pattern direction, then the second four need to be mirror images of the first four. Press the seams toward the darker fabric.

■ Lay the patches out in sequence and piece into five vertical strips. Press the seams in alternate directions and sew the five strips together.

One corner section, rotated repeat

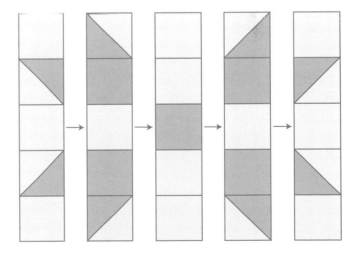

Nine-patch blocks

At its simplest, a nine-patch block consists of nine square patches—three across and three down—but it can also be made up of any number across and down that is a multiple of three. When the central square is left plain and the surrounding ones are halved or quartered diagonally, you get Star designs. Some blocks such as Grandma's Star and Flagstones have two entirely different patches to draft.

Sawtooth

Size of finished block: 12 in. square

The central diamond squares become very prominent as a chain on a quilt when the blocks are joined edge to edge. The grain on all the triangles should run along a short edge and on the squares from point to point.

■ Draft the templates (see page 160) and cut four large triangles each in red and yellow, four red squares, 16 green, and four yellow small triangles.

■ Piece the yellow/red triangle squares for the corners and press the seams toward the darker fabric.

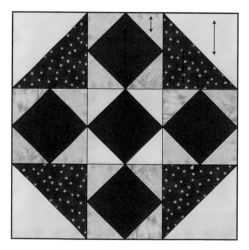

Two patches, alternating as shown

■ Sew the long edges of two small triangles to opposite sides of a square and press the seams away from the square. Repeat on the remaining two edges and press the seams outward. Do this on all five diamond squares.

■ Lay the patches out in sequence and piece into three vertical strips. Press the seams in alternate directions from strip to strip to avoid bulk at the seams. Sew the strips together and press all the vertical seams in the same direction across the block.

Nine Patch

Size of finished block: 12 in. square

When simple Nine Patch blocks are joined without sashing or alternating plain squares and with three diagonal squares in contrasting tones from the others, a diagonal chain will appear across the quilt.

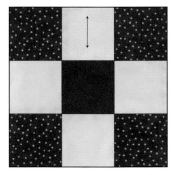

Four mirror-image corner patches, alternating with plain squares

■ Draft the template (see page 160) and cut four yellow squares, four patterned red squares, and one plain red square.

■ Lay the patches out in sequence and piece into three vertical strips. Press the seams in alternate directions. Sew the strips together and press all the vertical seams in the same direction across the block.

Shoo-fly

Size of finished block: 12 in. square

The corner patches of Shoo-fly are triangle squares. If blocks are joined edge to edge, an alternating color sequence of the squares and triangles from block to block will give a checked vertical/horizontal chain.

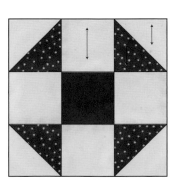

Four mirror-image corner patches, alternating with plain squares

■ Draft the templates (see page 160) and cut four triangles each in yellow and red, four yellow squares, and one red square.

■ Piece the yellow/red triangle squares and press the seams toward the darker fabric.

■ Lay the pieces out in sequence and piece into three vertical strips. Press the seams in alternate directions. Sew the strips together and press all the vertical seams in the same direction across the block.

Ohio Star, Swamp Patch

Size of finished block: 12 in. square

The corner patches—square on Ohio Star, triangle squares on Swamp Patch—turn into Broken Dishes when the blocks are joined without sashing, as on the cushion on page 109.

OHIO STAR

■ Draft the templates (see page 160) and cut eight red, four pale yellow, and four striped yellow triangles. (The grain line should run base to point on two of the inner small triangles and along the long edge of the other two.) Also cut four pale yellow squares and one checked yellow center square.

■ Lay pale yellow triangles on red triangles, and the remaining red triangles on striped triangles, and stitch along one short edge to make eight larger triangles. Press the seams towards the darker fabric. Piece into four triangle squares, being careful to match the centres.

■ Lay the patches out in sequence. Piece into three vertical strips and press the seams in alternate directions. Sew the strips together and press all the vertical seams in the same direction across the block.

SWAMP PATCH

■ There are two sizes of triangles on Swamp Patch, with the grain lines running in different directions. If you are using a striped fabric, then the grain line should run from base to point on two of the inner small triangles and along the long edge of the other two.

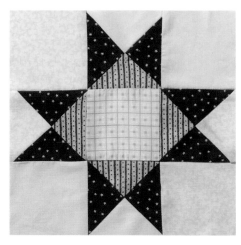

OHIO STAR

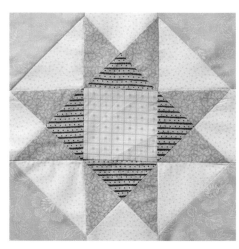

SWAMP PATCH

■ Draft the templates (see page 160) and cut eight yellow, four dotted cream, and four striped small triangles, two large triangles each in dotted cream and beige, and one checked center square.

■ Piece the large dotted cream/beige triangles into triangle squares. Press the seams toward the darker fabric.

■ Piece the small yellow/striped and yellow/dotted cream triangles into larger triangles as for Ohio Star, and press the seams toward the darker color. Piece into four triangle squares, being careful to match the centers.

■ Lay the patches out in sequence. Piece into three vertical strips, and press the seams in alternate directions. Sew the strips together and press all the vertical seams in the same direction across the block.

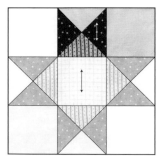

One patch rotated, with plain corner squares

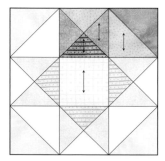

One patch rotated, with triangle squares in the corners

Grandma's Star

Size of finished block: 12 in. square

This block requires careful drafting, because there are two sizes of tall triangles to piece.

■ Draft the templates (see page 160) and cut eight thin white triangles (mirror image), four large green triangles, and 10 squares each in two contrasting colors.

■ Piece the squares into five Four Patch blocks (see page 10).

■ Lay a thin white triangle along one long edge of each large green triangle and stitch together. Press the seam toward the darker fabric. Sew a mirror-image thin triangle to the other long edge and press the seam toward the darker fabric again.

■ Lay the patches out in sequence. Piece into three vertical strips and press the seams in alternate directions. Sew the strips together, being careful to match the points in the center, and press all the vertical seams in the same direction across the block.

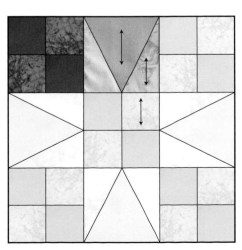

Two patches, alternating as shown

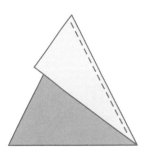
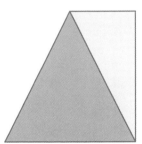
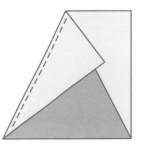
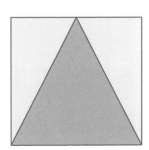

Cat's Cradle

Size of finished block: 12 in. square

The six identical triangle patches are rotated to make the design, with the large squares forming a diagonal through the block.

■ Draft the templates (see page 160) and cut six large triangles and three squares in patterned red, six small red triangles, and 18 small yellow triangles.

■ Piece six small red/yellow triangle squares and press the seams toward the red fabric. Place one short edge of a small yellow triangle on one red edge of each triangle square and stitch together. Sew another yellow triangle to the remaining red edge of the triangle square. Press the seams toward the long edge of the new large triangle.

■ Sew each pieced large triangle to a red patterned triangle to make six triangle squares, being careful not to lose the points.

■ Lay the patches out in sequence. Piece into three vertical strips and press the seams in alternate directions. Sew the strips together and press all the vertical seams in the same direction across the block.

One patch rotated, with plain squares forming a diagonal chain

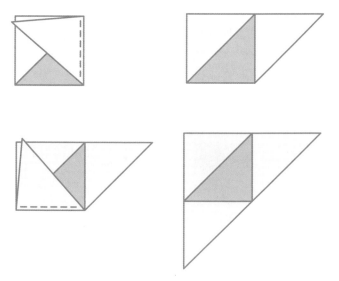

Air Castle

Size of finished block: 12 in. square

This block has four identical triangle squares and four split triangle squares rotated around a central diamond square. Grain lines vary but it is important to cut the center square with the grain line running vertically to avoid distortion and stretch.

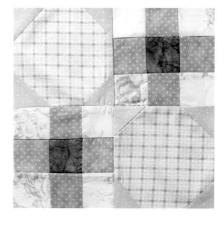

■ Draft the templates (see page 160) and cut four large triangles each in plum, pink, and white sprigged fabric, four medium-sized triangles each in white sprig and pink floral fabric, four small triangles in white sprigged fabric, and one plum square.

■ Piece together the small white-sprigged triangles and the plum square. Press the seams on all pieces towards the darker fabric. Piece the medium-sized triangles in pairs to make four large triangles and sew these to the pink fabric triangles to make triangle squares. Piece the large plum/white sprigged triangle squares.

■ Piece the patches into three vertical strips and sew the strips together.

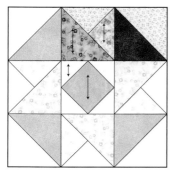

Two patches, alternating as shown, around a central diamond square

---

Flagstones

Size of finished block: 12 in. square

Flagstones consists of a simple Nine Patch and an octagon, which is made into a square by filling in each corner with a triangle. Although this block is easy to draft, it can be difficult to match the octagon seams to the nine-patch squares.

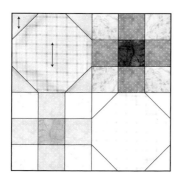

Two quarter blocks, alternating as shown

■ Draft the templates (see page 160). For the two nine-patch squares, cut eight green, eight cream, and two mauve squares. For the two octagon patches, cut two checked fabric octagons and eight pale triangles.

■ Piece the two nine-patch quarters (see page 29).

■ Piece the long edge of the triangles to the cut edges of the octagons (so that the grain matches) and press the seams away from the octagons.

■ Piece each nine-patch quarter to an octagon patch. Press the seams in alternate directions. Sew the two strips together and press all the vertical seams in the same direction across the quilt.

Gentleman's Fancy

Size of finished block: 12 in.

This block is drafted as a Nine Patch (page 29), but it is built up from the center, around the central square, and not in strips. The small triangles have the grain line along their long edge, while on the larger ones the grain line follows a short edge.

■ Draft the templates (see page 160) and cut four small triangles each in cream sprigged and dotted cream fabric, eight small pink sprigged triangles, four large triangles each in plum and cream dot, and one pink sprigged center square.

■ Sew the long side of one small cream sprigged triangle to each side of the center square to form a square "on point" and press the seams outward. Sew the long side of each large plum triangle to one side of the square on point and press the seams outward.

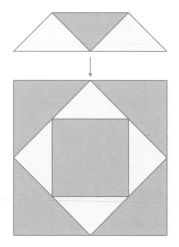

■ Sew a small pink sprigged triangle to each short side of a small dotted cream triangle and press the seams toward the darker fabric. Sew these pieces to the square, being careful to keep the points matched, and press the seams outward. Finally, sew on the large dotted cream corner triangles.

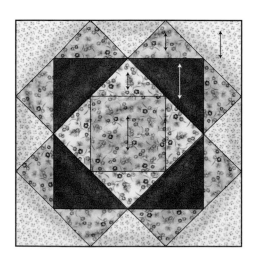

Bright Star

Size of finished block: 12 in. square

Bright Star looks like a four-patch block, as it has four identical patches rotated to make the design, but each quarter is drafted as a nine-patch block.

■ Draft the templates (see page 160) and cut eight blue and 12 yellow small triangles, four medium-sized mid-mauve triangles, and four large lilac triangles.

■ Piece eight blue/yellow triangle squares and assemble in pairs. Sew one short edge of a small yellow triangle to one end of each pair. Press the seams toward the darker fabric to avoid show-through.

■ Piece to one short edge of a mid-mauve triangle to make a large triangle. Sew each large pieced triangle to a large lilac triangle to make four triangle squares.

■ Lay the patches out in sequence. Piece into two vertical strips and press the seams in alternate directions. Sew the strips together, being careful to match up the center points.

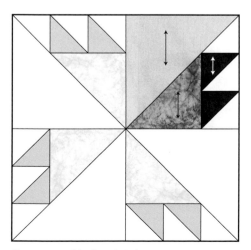

One quarter block, rotated

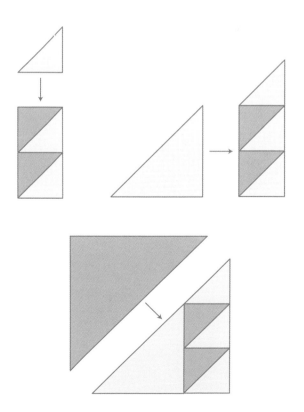

Barn Fence

Size of finished block: 12 in. square

Barn Fence is a simple Nine Patch with patches made up of strips. The strips do not have to be of even width, so this is a good design for using up scraps. Blocks are generally joined edge to edge without sashing, to give a woven effect.

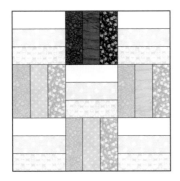

One patch, rotated

■ Draft the templates (see page 160). Piece strips together to make nine patches—four in one colorway and five in another. Press the seams toward the darker fabric.

■ Sew the patches together in three vertical strips, and press the seams in alternate directions. Sew the strips together and press all the vertical seams in the same direction across the block.

London Roads

Size of finished block: 12 in. square

London Roads has four patches made of strips (as Barn Fence). Corner patches are quartered diagonally, and the center square is plain. The strips can be random widths. Here, the central bars are a similar color to the adjoining dark corner triangles, so vertical arrows have appeared.

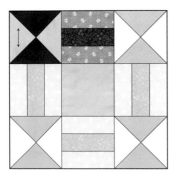

Two patches, alternating as shown, around a plain center square

■ Draft the templates (see page 160) and cut one green center square. Cut eight small triangles each in blue and green and piece into eight identical large blue/green triangles. Join in pairs to make four triangle squares. Press the seams toward the darker fabric. Piece four patches from strips, as for Barn Fence.

■ Lay out the patches in sequence. Piece into three vertical strips and press the seams in alternate directions. Sew the strips together and press the vertical seams in the same direction across the block.

Pine Tree

Size of finished block: 15 in. square

When Pine Tree is combined with alternating plain squares, the tree shape is retained. If joining blocks edge to edge, make the trunk thinner, so that the pines look separated by intricate triangle-square sashing across the quilt top.

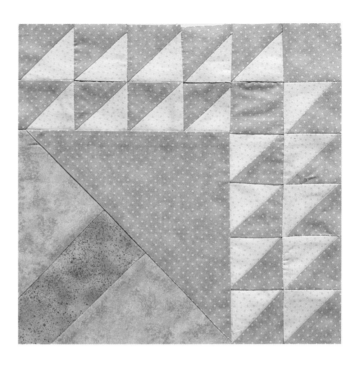

■ Draft the templates (see page 160) and cut 18 small triangles each in cream and green, two green squares, one large green triangle, two smaller blue triangles, and a fawn trunk.

■ Sew each blue triangle to the trunk along one short edge to make a triangle, and piece into a triangle square with the large green triangle.

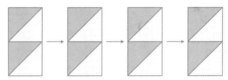

■ Piece the small cream/green triangles into 18 triangle squares. Sew eight triangle squares together into vertical pairs and press the seams toward the darker fabric. Piece the pairs into a strip and sew to the top of the large triangle square. Press the seams toward the trunk.

■ Sew the remaining small triangle squares together into two vertical strips for the right-hand edge of the block with a green square as the second patch down on the left-hand strip and as the top patch on right-hand strip.

■ Sew the two vertical strips to the block and press the seams towards the trunk.

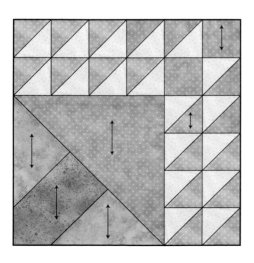

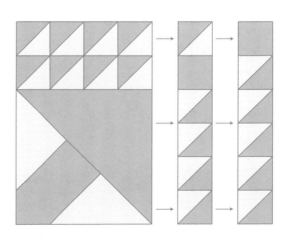

Seven-patch blocks

Seven-patch blocks have seven patches across and down, so it is best not make them too small. Some, such as Bear's Paw, have very distinctive shapes and look better with sashing, while others, such as Checkers, can be pieced edge to edge.

Bear's Paw

Size of finished block: 14 in. square

Four identical patches are separated by a central cross. All triangles point outward, so must be level. Separate blocks with sashing to preserve the distinctive shape.

■ Draft the templates (see page 160) and cut 16 small triangles each in bright red and pale green, four small pale green squares for the corners, one small black square for the center, four large squares in gray, and four oblongs in yellow.

■ Piece the 16 red/pale green triangles into triangle squares and press the seams toward the darker fabric. Assemble into four sets of mirror-image pairs.

■ Lay the patches out in sequence and piece the red edge of one of each pair of triangle squares to one edge of a large gray square. Press the seams toward the square. Sew a small pale green square to the red edge of each of the remaining pairs. Press the seams toward the darker fabric.

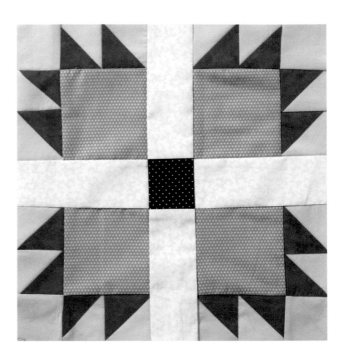

■ Join these strips to an adjacent edge, so that the pale green square at the end of the strip forms the corner. Press the seams toward the gray square.

■ Lay out in sequence and piece into vertical strips, with the yellow oblongs in between. Press the seams toward the oblongs and trim the seams to avoid show-through. Piece the central strip with the black square in its center. Sew the three vertical strips together and press the seams toward the center.

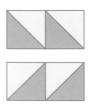

One patch, rotated around center square and strip

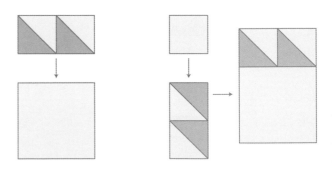

Checkers

Size of finished block: 15¾ in. square

Alternate the sequence of small squares to avoid piecing the same colors next to each other, or use different colors.

■ Draft the templates (see page 160) and cut 16 red and 17 yellow small squares, and four large gray squares.

■ Piece six yellow/red squares into pairs and the rest into strips of seven squares; two of the seven-square strips should have a yellow patch at each end, one should have red at each end. Press the seams toward the dark color.

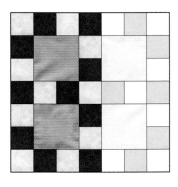

■ Lay out in sequence and join the pairs of squares to the gray squares to make two broad strips.

■ Assemble these five strips and press seams in the same direction across the block.

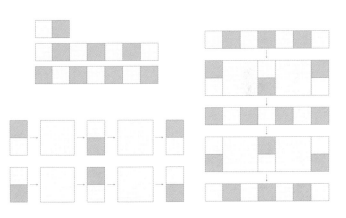

Prickly Pear

Size of finished block: 15¾ in. square

This block is best made fairly large with the outer triangles in strong colors. It is simple to piece but can be confusing, so it is essential to arrange the pieces before assembling.

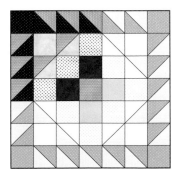

■ Draft the templates (see page 160) and cut 28 gray, 20 black and eight yellow triangles, and four squares each in black, red, and yellow, one in gray, eight in white.

■ Make eight yellow/gray and 20 black/gray triangle squares.

■ Lay out the patches in sequence and assemble them into seven vertical strips. Press the seams in alternate directions strip by strip and sew the strips together. Press the vertical seams in the same direction across the block.

Hexagons, diamonds, and stars

Hexagons and diamonds are traditionally pieced by hand over light paper templates so are perfect for using scraps. They must be made with even-weave cottons or silks, because synthetics will stretch out of shape and will not lie flat. Star blocks can either be pieced by hand over papers or machine stitched. They are pieced from the center outward—first the stars are pieced and then the triangles and squares are added to the edges to make the blocks square.

Grandmother's Flower Garden

Size of finished rosette: 5½ in.

In this pattern, individual rosettes are made up of a central hexagon with six matching or random petal hexagons around it. You will also need extra hexagons (white with pink flowers in the example shown here) to fill in the gaps when the rosettes are joined together. Alternatively, make large rosettes with six inner and 12 outer petals.

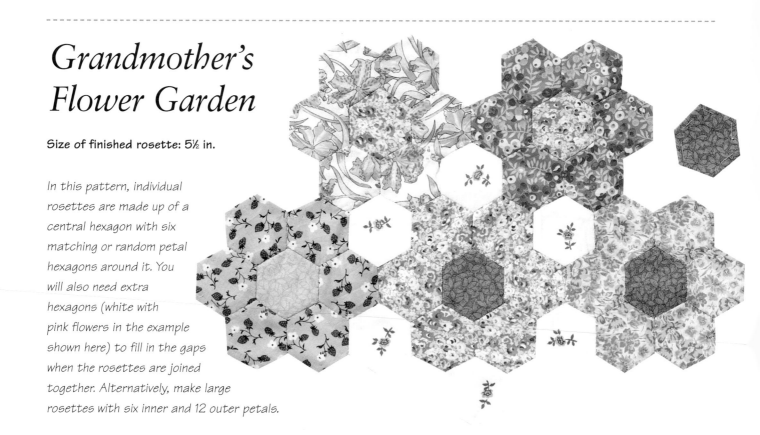

■ To make a template, draw a circle with a 1-in. radius and mark the edge at 60° intervals. Draw a line between these marks. This is the template for the backing papers. Now add a ¼-in. turning allowance to each edge and make a second template for fabric cutting. It is best to make templates from cardboard or plastic, because a quilt project requires hundreds of hexagons.

■ For each rosette, cut seven backing papers from the first template, and six fabric shapes in one color and one fabric shape in a contrasting color for the center from the second template.

■ Pin the papers to the wrong side of the fabric hexagons, turn the edges over and baste; try not to knot the thread, but if you do, leave the knots on the right side of the fabric to make the basting easier to remove.

■ Take the center hexagon and place right sides together with a rosette hexagon. Whipstitch along one edge and then flatten. Take a second rosette and again, right sides together, whipstitch it to an adjacent edge of the center hexagon. Flatten and then pinch together the two rosette hexagons to stitch the adjoining seam. Continue until the rosette is complete.

■ You will need extra hexagons (white on the example shown here) to fill in the spaces between the rosettes when you come to sew them together.

■ Leave all the backing papers in place until the whole project is complete. There is no need to press the patchwork because the basting will have made a good crease over the time it takes to work a quilt top.

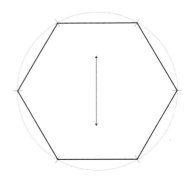

■ When finished, remove the basting stitches and backing papers; you may find that you have caught the edges of the papers in your stitching, so be gentle when removing them.

Pentagon Rosette

Size of finished rosette: 5½ in.

Pentagon Rosettes can be used in conjunction with Grandmother's Flower Garden rosettes, since the outside edges are the same shape.

■ Draft a hexagon template in the same way as for Grandmother's Flower Garden, but extend two edges to twice the length of the other sides.

■ Piece with papers, sewing the shapes together one by one along their long edges.

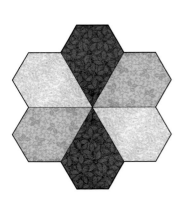

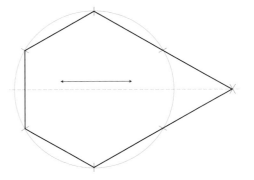

Six-Pointed Star

Size of finished block: 8 in.

Length of finished diamond: 4 in.

This design can be worked by hand over papers and the resulting hexagons joined into large rosettes. However, it is also easy to piece by machine, as described here.

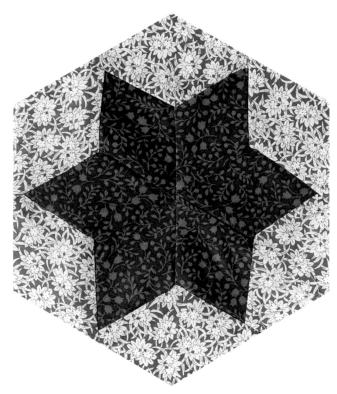

■ Draw a circle with a radius of 4 in. and mark the edge at 60° intervals. Draw lines radiating from the center to each of the marked points. Divide one segment in half and draw lines at 60° from the circle edge to the segment lines. All four sides will be the same length. Make a template, adding a ¼-in. seam allowance all around.

■ Cut six diamonds in each of two colors. Place two diamonds of the same color right sides together and stitch along one edge—but do not secure the ends of the seam, as you will need to undo the stitching at one end by about ¼ in. later. Press the seam. Take a third diamond in the same color and stitch it to the second edge of the first diamond.

■ Make another set of three diamonds in the same color, and press the seams in the same direction as the first set. Pin at the center and piece the two halves together, stitching slowly over the seams to keep the points true.

■ Place an outer diamond (in the second color) in position and stitch from the outside toward the seam of the star. Stop stitching when you reach the seam, and break off. Undo about ¼ in. of the star seam and bring the edge of the diamonds level. Stitch from the seam to the outer edge of the diamond. Press the seams outward, away from the star—you'll find that the tenting will flatten. Repeat all the way around.

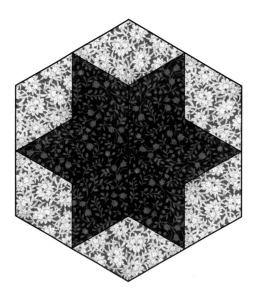

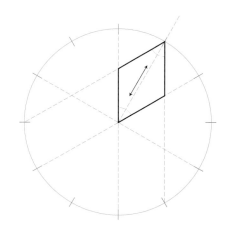

Tumbling Blocks

Size of finished block: 4 in. wide

Length of finished diamond: 4 in.

This design could be worked by hand over papers or machine stitched, as described here. To create the 3-D effect, choose fabrics with strong light, mid, and dark tones.

The templates are drafted in the same way as for Six-Pointed Star, but the diamonds are pieced in threes, with mid and dark diamonds pieced to adjacent edges of a light diamond. The resulting hexagon blocks are then joined first into rows, and then row upon row.

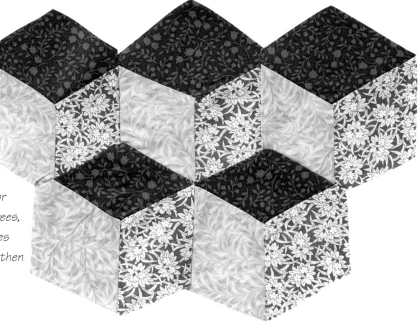

■ Make a diamond template in the same way as for Six-Pointed Star and cut three diamonds—one light, one mid-tone, and one dark. Stitch the pale diamond to the mid-toned diamond along one edge, starting and stopping the seam about ¼ in. from the ends.

■ Place the dark diamond above the first two and stitch the dark diamond to the pale one from the outside toward the seam of the pale and mid diamonds, starting and stopping about ¼ in. from the ends. Bring the dark diamond edge level with the mid-toned one and stitch toward the point, again starting and stopping about ¼ in. from the ends. Once several blocks have been pieced together, press the seams toward the darker fabrics. You'll find that the tenting will flatten.

■ To join several tumbling blocks together, first piece two together, mid-toned to pale edge, starting and stopping about ¼ in. from the ends. Next, add a third block above these two, right sides together, stitching a pale edge to a dark edge, and starting and stopping ¼ in. from the ends as before. Add a fourth block and continue, always with just two edges to stitch.

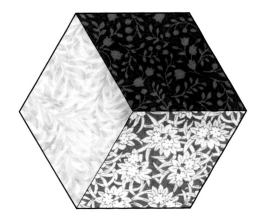

Back

Front

Eight-Pointed Star

Size of finished block: 13 in.

Length of finished diamond: 7 in.

This design can be worked by hand over papers or by machine, as described here. The Star is pieced first, and then the edge triangles and corner squares are added.

■ Draw a circle with a 5¾-in. radius and mark the edge at 45° intervals. Draw lines radiating from the center to each of the marked points. Divide one segment in half and draw lines at 45° to the segment lines. You can now draw in the block edges so they are level with the tips of the star. The grain line should be along the long edge of the triangles. On the diamonds it can run along the length so any pattern direction on the fabric looks even. Add a ¼-in. seam allowance to all templates.

■ Cut four diamonds in each of two colors and four triangles and squares in cream.

■ Piece the diamonds in contrasting pairs, and join the pairs in groups of two to make the two halves of the star. Don't secure the seam ends as you will need to undo the stitching at one end by about ¼ in. To avoid bulk at the center, press the seams so they lie in opposite directions at the center. Lay the two halves of the star right sides together and stitch, being careful to match the center points.

■ With right sides together, and working with the star uppermost, stitch a corner square along one edge of a diamond to the seam, stopping the seam ¼ in. from the end near the star seam. Undo about ¼ in. of the star seam and bring the edge of the next diamond and square level. Stitch from the seam to the outer edge of the square. Press the seams outward, away from the star—you'll find that the tenting will flatten. Repeat all the way around.

■ Insert the triangles in the same way. Press the seams away from the star.

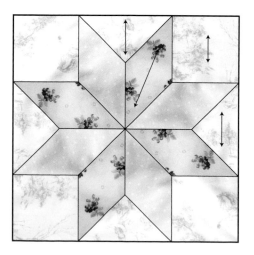

Star of the East

Size of finished block: 13 in. square

Length of finished diamond: 7 in.

This block has split diamonds in contrasting colors, and works best with sashing or as a central medallion.

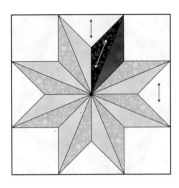

■ Draft a star within an 5¾-in. radius circle, as for Eight-Pointed Star (see page 44), then divide the diamond shape in half, from point to point to make the split diamond template. Piece the diamond halves together first and press the seams toward the darker fabric. Then piece the remainder of the block in the same way as for Eight-Pointed Star. There will be a lot of bulk in the center, so take extra care to keep the points true.

Star upon Stars

Size of finished block: 13 in. square

Length of finished diamond: 3½ in.

Each point is made of four, nine, or 16 diamonds. The pillow project on page 108 has nine diamonds per point.

■ Draft a star within an 5¾-in. radius circle, as for Eight-Pointed Star (see page 44) and then quarter the diamond to make the small diamond templates. Draft the corner squares and triangles in the center of each side as for Eight-Pointed Star.

■ Cut eight dark blue, eight cream sprig, and 16 mid-blue diamonds, four yellow triangles, and four yellow squares.

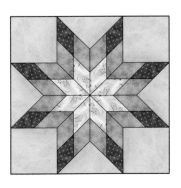

■ Piece eight cream/ mid blue and eight mid blue/dark blue diamonds in identical pairs and press the seams toward the darker fabric. With right sides together, stitch alternate pairs together to make eight identical large diamonds. Pin at the seam intersections to keep the points true and stitch together to make the central eight-point star.

■ Assemble the block with the squares at the corners and triangles along edges in the same way as for Eight-Pointed Star (see page 44).

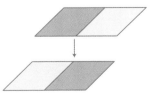

Kaleidoscope

Size of finished block: 11½ in. square

This block is divided into eight segments like Eight-Pointed Star, but it is much easier to piece as the segments fill the block.

■ Divide the block through the center into 45° angles, as for Eight-Pointed Star, and draw lines to the edges of the block. Draw a straight line across each corner between the marked points. The cones have the grain line running along their length; on the corner triangles, the grain line is parallel to the edges of the block. Add a ¼-in. seam allowance to each template.

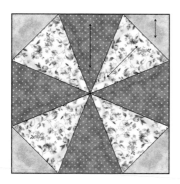

■ Cut four cone shapes each in blue dots and white sprig, and four pale blue corner triangles.

■ Piece each triangle to a white sprig cone and press the seams outward. Piece this to a blue dot cone to make quarter blocks. Piece two quarter blocks, and then sew the two halves together across the center, being careful to match the points. The seams should be in alternate directions to avoid bulk at the center.

Spider's Web

Size of finished block: 11½ in. square

This can be made with alternating striped and plain cones. The stripes do not have to be of even width. The diagonal cones are single pieces of fabric, without corner triangles.

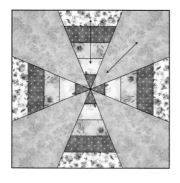

■ Cut four solid fabric blue cones and four striped ones made up of 1½-in. strips.

■ Assemble as for Kaleidoscope.

Attic Windows

Size of finished block: 9½ in. square

To achieve the 3-D effect, use fabrics that contrast strongly in tone for the "frames." The "window panes" could all be made from different fabrics or even from small appliquéd blocks.

■ To draft templates, draw a 4¾-in. square for one quarter block. The frame is 1¼ in. wide with a 45° angle. Add a ¼-in. seam allowance to each template.

■ Cut four patterned squares and four rectangles each of pale and dark fabric. The pale rectangles are mirror image of the dark ones.

■ With right sides together, stitch a pale rectangle to a square, stopping ¼ in. before the angle. Next, stitch a dark rectangle, again stopping ¼ in. before the angle. Pull the angle edges level and miter the corner (see page 171). Press the seams outward, away from the central squares.

■ Piece the patches in vertical pairs and press the seams in alternate directions. Sew these pairs together and press all the vertical seams in the same direction across the quilt.

Curved blocks

Curved patches can form part of any block. The ones shown are all four-patch blocks (Drunkard's Path is subdivided into 16 patches), apart from the Fan blocks, which are one-patch blocks. The curves are pieced first and the resulting patches assembled into vertical strips. If there are several curved pieces in a patch, the smallest, inner curves should be pieced first.

Robbing Peter to Pay Paul

Size of finished block: 14 in. square

This design is similar to Drunkard's Path (see page 50), but is trickier to piece as all the patches have curves to match up on every side.

■ Draw an 7-in. square on graph paper. Using a compass, draw a quarter circle halfway along one edge, using a 3½-in. radius. Add a ¼-in. seam allowance all around each template.

■ Cut two of each shape in two different colors.

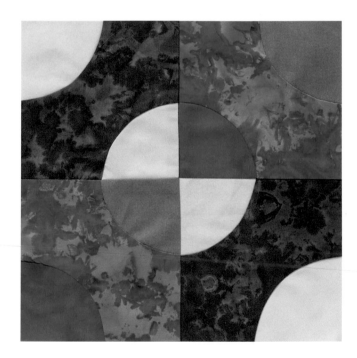

■ In the same way as for Drunkard's Path (see page 50), fold each piece in half diagonally along its curve and crease the center mark to make it easier to match up. Pin and piece one side of a patch, press the seam away from the quarter circle, and then piece the second quarter circle.

■ Pin and piece the upper and lower patches together and press the seams in alternate directions. Sew the two sections together and press all the vertical seams in the same direction across the quilt.

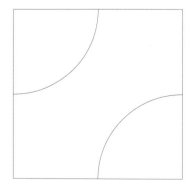

Four-patch block in two colorways

Fair Play

Size of finished block: 14 in. square

Although the individual patches are similar to Drunkard's Path (see page 50), the design is much less forgiving as the two curves need to be cut and pieced very accurately so that they meet precisely when joined.

■ Draw an 7-in. square on graph paper. Using a compass, draw a quarter circle halfway along one edge, using a 3½-in. radius. Mark a second ring 1¼ in. farther along. Add a ¼-in. seam allowance all around each template.

■ Cut two of each shape in two different colors.

■ In the same way as for Drunkard's Path (see page 50), fold each piece in half diagonally along its curve and crease the center mark to make it easier to match up. Pin and piece the center segments first and press the seams away from the center. Repeat with the outer rings. If a dark fabric is being pressed toward a paler one, you may need to trim the darker seam allowance so that it doesn't show through on the front.

■ Pin and piece the upper and lower patches together and press the seams in alternate directions. Sew the two sections together and press all the vertical seams in the same direction across the quilt top.

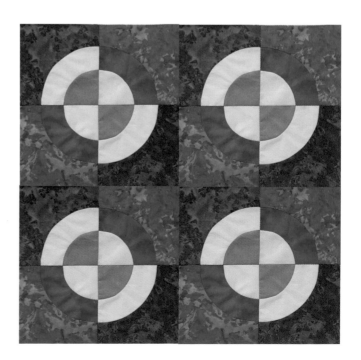

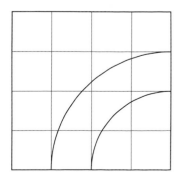

Four-patch block in two colorways

Drunkard's Path

Size of finished block: 19 in. square

This is a repeating block of 16 patches, with only two shapes and three colors. Since a double-bed quilt would need five blocks across and five down, making 400 of each shape, be sure to make sturdy templates that won't get damaged with so much use.

■ Draw a 4¾-in. square on graph paper. Using a compass, draw a quarter circle two-thirds of the way along one edge, using a radius of 3⅛ in. Cut out and glue the pieces to cardboard, adding a seam allowance of ¼ in. all the way around each piece.

■ Cut eight blue and eight yellow squares with concave curves, and eight blue and eight cream quarter circles.

■ If the fabric has a directional pattern, as shown here, cut half the shapes with the right side of the fabric facing you and half with the wrong side facing. The shapes are simple but the pattern repeats can be very confusing, so lay the 32 pieces out in sequence, alternating lights and darks, before piecing, keeping the fabric direction uniform across the block.

■ Fold each square and quarter circle in half diagonally and crease mid curve as a matching guide. Place a quarter circle on a square, right sides together, and pin along the crease with the pin head facing outward so that you can remove it easily as you stitch.

Pull the straight edges of each side level and pin. Add just a couple more pins to the curve. Turn over, as it is easier to stitch the stretchy concave curve to the quarter circle curve. As you stitch (slowly), tug gently at the top fabric to keep the fabric edges level and make the curves fit.

■ Press, gently ironing the quarter circle flat. You can nudge the curve into shape with the tip of the iron from the front.

■ When all the patches are pieced and pressed lay them out in sequence again and piece in vertical strips. Alternate the seam directions from strip to strip to avoid bulk at the seams. Sew the strips together and press all the vertical seams in the same direction across the quilt.

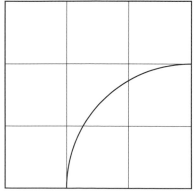

One patch, rotated repeat

Mary's Fan

Size of finished block: 10 in. square

This is a one-patch block. Traditionally, it was made into a quilt top with alternating plain blocks, giving scope for hand-quilted designs in each. It could also be assembled with sashing strips.

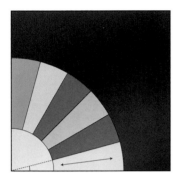

■ Draw a 10-in. square and mark two rings with radii of 3 in. and 7 in. Divide the outer ring into six segments at 15° intervals. Make templates, adding a ¼-in. seam allowance all around. The segments have grain lines running lengthwise.

■ Piece the segments and press the seams toward the darker fabric. Fold the pieces to mark the center points and piece as for Drunkard's Path (see page 50), working the small curve first and pressing the seams outward.

Broken Circles

Size of finished block: 14 in. square

Size of each finished patch: 7 in. square

This is a four-patch block, with two different patches to draft. The top left and lower right quarter blocks have rings with radii of 1½ in. and 4 in. On the top right and lower left quarter blocks, the radii of the rings are 2¾ in. and 6 in. Make templates, adding a ¼-in. seam allowance all around.

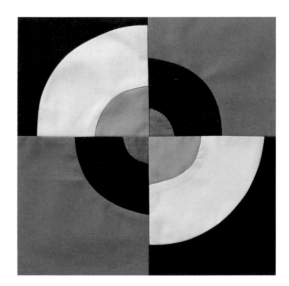

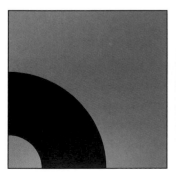
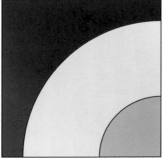

Two patches, mirror images

■ Cut two of each shape in different colors.

■ Fold, pin, piece, and press the inner rings first, as for Drunkard's Path (see page 50), then piece the outer rings.

■ Pin and piece the upper and lower patches together, pressing the seams in opposite directions. Join the two sections to complete the block and press all the vertical seams in the same direction across the quilt.

Grandmother's Fan

Size of finished block: 10 in. square

This is a one-patch block, similar to Mary's Fan but put together differently. The fans are assembled and stitched onto a backing, and then the centers are applied. This makes it a sturdy, hardwearing block, and one suitable for using different weights and recycled fabrics because the strain is taken by the backing fabric, not the piecing.

■ Cut a 11-in. backing square. (You can trim it to size once finished.)

■ Draw a 10-in. square and mark two rings with radii of 3½ in. and 8¼ in. Divide the outer ring into five segments at 18° intervals. Make templates, adding a ¼-in. seam allowance all around (unless you are working by machine, in which case the quarter circle does not need a seam allowance on the curved edge).

■ Cut the segments with the grain lines running lengthwise. Piece the segments and press the seams towards the darker fabric. Pin onto the backing square.

■ If you are working by hand, turn the curved edges under and slipstitch to the backing fabric, gently undoing the seams a little to tuck the turning allowance under. Stitch the quarter circle in place.

Hand finished

Machine stitched

■ If you are machine stitching, turn the segment edges under straight to form a point and topstitch, gently undoing the seams a little to tuck the turning allowance under. Topstitch the segment seams, too. Pin and satin stitch the curved edge of the quarter circle (stitch width 4).

Dresden Plate

Size of finished block: 15¾ in. square

This particular design has 20 segments, so it has the same angles (18°) as Grandmother's Fan (see page 52). You can use the same template, reducing the radii to 1½ in. and 7 in. Dresden Plate can, however, be made with any number of segments. For 24 divisions, use the template for Mary's Fan (page 51), with the segments having an angle of 15°; for 16 divisions, the angle would be 22.5°. The "Plate" is stitched onto a backing fabric and the central circle applied last.

■ Cut a 17-in. backing square. (You can trim it to size once finished.)

■ To make the template, draw a 8-in. square (one-quarter of the block) and mark two rings with radii of 1½in. and 7 in. Divide the outer ring into five segments at 18° intervals. Make a segment template, adding a

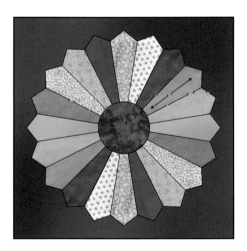

¼-in. seam allowance all around. The segments have the grain lines running lengthwise. The center circle has a 1¾-in. radius; no seam allowance is added if it is satin stitched in place, but if you are working by hand it will need a ¼-in. turning allowance.

■ Cut and piece all the segments to form a ring and, pressing from the back, press all the seams in the same direction. Pin this big ring to the backing fabric and topstitch it in place, turning the curves under to form points. Then topstitch the segment seams.

■ Pin and satin stitch the centre circle in place (stitch width 4) or turn the allowance under and slipstitch by hand.

Foundation blocks

Foundation blocks are stitched onto a backing fabric to keep the lines true. They have a center patch which is pieced around and around. They are good blocks to choose if you are using recycled fabrics of different strengths, as the strain will be taken by the backing fabric rather than the seams. These blocks can be worked without a backing fabric, but if they are made any larger than 13 in. there is a risk of "tenting," which means that the centers will bulge and distort.

Log Cabin and Courthouse Steps

Size of finished block: 11½ in. square

Size of each finished strip: 1¼ in. wide

These two blocks are constructed in a very similar way—the difference being that in Log Cabin adjacent sides of the central square are in light or dark tones, while in Courthouse Steps opposite sides of the central square are light or dark.

Vary the fabric of the outer strips of the blocks, so that dark can be placed next to dark without the risk of the same fabric being on the edge of the neighboring block.

For a large double-sized quilt, you will need about eight blocks across and down.

■ Cut the center square 2 in. square and the strips 1¾ in. wide—this includes the ¼-in. seam allowance. The longest strip required is 28 in.

■ Cut a piece of backing cotton about 13½ in. square, fold it in quarters and then diagonally, and press. The crease lines will act as a piecing guide to keep the block square. Pin the center square (which is traditionally red to represent the hearth in the Log Cabin) in place.

Log Cabin

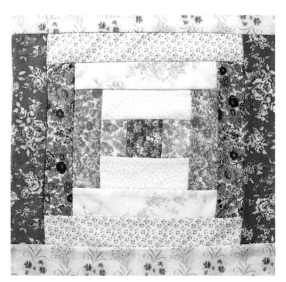

Courthouse Steps

Log Cabin

■ With right sides together, piece the palest strip to one side of the center square, trimming to length as you go. When you flip the strip over, it will be right side up. Press flat, turn the block clockwise, and add the second pale strip. Press, turn the piece clockwise again, add a dark fabric, and then repeat. It is best to iron the block as you piece. Continue building the block by adding pale and dark strips around and around.

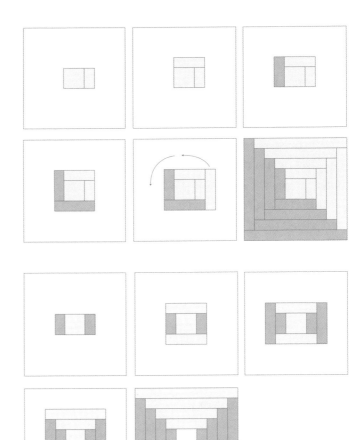

Courthouse Steps

■ With right sides together, piece two dark strips to opposite sides of the center square. Then piece two pale strips to the top and lower edges. Continue adding dark strips to the sides and light strips to the top and bottom, until the block is the required size.

Log Cabin settings

■ Different patterns become apparent with different placements and rotations of the blocks.

■ Light and Dark has the blocks all in the same direction across the quilt.

■ In Straight Furrow, the neighboring block is rotated 180°. It is best to make two sets of blocks with different fabrics on the outside edges to avoid identical fabrics being pieced together.

■ Barn Raising needs an even number of blocks across and down to make it symmetrical. It is best to make two sets of blocks with different fabrics on the outside edges to avoid identical fabrics being pieced together. Lay out in sequence from the center, with all the darks together, then continue as Straight Furrow.

Light and Dark

Straight Furrow

Barn Raising

Pineapple

Size of finished block: 12 in. square

Size of finished strip: 1 in. wide

Working around a central square, piece four pale and then four dark strips, the pales horizontally and vertically, the darks across the diagonals. Cut the strip lengths as you proceed. You may need to trim away excess fabric from the dark strips to avoid show-through. You could draft the design on paper and cut templates (adding a ¼-in. seam allowance all around) for each of the strips.

■ Cut the center square 2½ in. square and the strips 1½ in. wide—this includes the ¼-in. seam allowances. The longest pale and dark strips required (two of each) are 52 in.

■ Cut a piece of backing cotton about 14 in. square, fold it in quarters and then diagonally, and press. The crease lines will act as a piecing guide to keep the block true. Pin the center square in place.

■ With right sides together, piece four pale strips to the edges of the center square, trimming to length as you proceed. The strips should overlap by about ¼ in. at the

ends. Flip over the strips as you proceed, so they are right side up, and press flat.

■ Piece four dark fabrics diagonally, again overlapping the ends by about ¼ in. Press.

■ The next four pale strips do not need to overlap, but should just reach the outer edges of the dark fabric. They are placed horizontally and vertically.

■ Continue by piecing four dark fabrics diagonally.

■ Continue around and around, alternating light and dark. A further two dark strips will be needed on the corners. Finally, trim the block square.

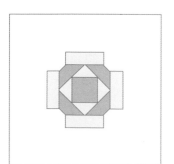
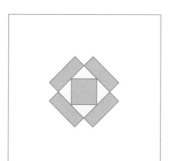
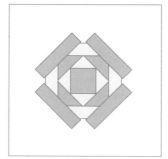
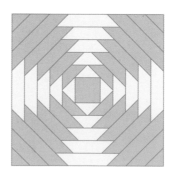

Snail Trail

Size of finished block: 13 in. square

This block requires templates for the triangles, with the grain directions marked. The grain must run vertically to avoid distortion and stretch, and the grain is different from one size of triangle to the next. Using striped fabrics will increase the swirling effect when the blocks are joined together.

■ Draw a 13-in. square, with an 3⅛-in. square in the center, quartered. Draw a square on point around this, touching the corners of the center patch, then a square, and so on. Add a ¼-in. seam allowance around each template.

■ Cut a piece of backing cotton about 15 in. square, fold it in quarters and then diagonally, and press. These crease lines will act as a piecing guide to keep the block true.

■ Piece the center Four Patch, press it, and pin it to the center of the backing fabric.

■ With right sides together, piece the two smallest pale triangles to opposite sides of the center Four Patch, then piece the two smallest dark triangles to the top and lower edges. Flip back the triangles and press flat.

■ Turn the block counterclockwise. Piece pale triangles to the sides and dark triangles to the top and bottom. Press. Repeat until the block is complete.

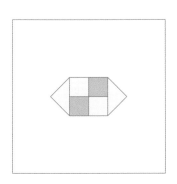
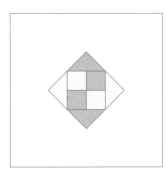
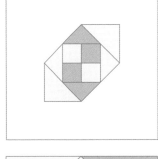
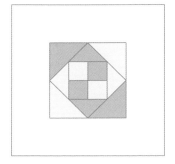
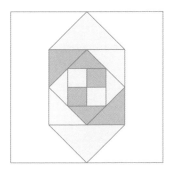
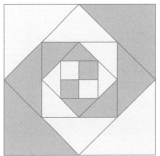

Patchwork borders

When the same blocks are repeated across an entire quilt, there is no need for a border pattern. If, however, your quilt would benefit from a border, there are several distinct patterns to choose from, as well as part blocks that can be used as borders—Bear's Paw, Goose Tracks, and Bright Star work well, and Old Maid's Puzzle has two different quarter patches, either of which could be repeated around a quilt of that design. Draft the templates for borders as explained on page 160.

Sawtooth

Size of finished patch: 3 in.

Sawtooth has squares made up of two differently colored triangles pieced in the same orientation, while for Reverse Sawtooth the squares are rotated. A double row of Sawtooth is effective since the triangles become split diamonds, while a double row of Reverse Sawtooth is, in fact, Fly or Broken Dishes. Using more than two colors can change the appearance of Sawtooth.

Sawtooth

Reverse Sawtooth

Sawtooth using more than one color

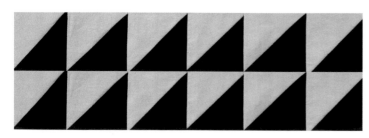

Double row of Sawtooth

Chevron

Size of finished patch: 3 in. (7.5 cm) square

This uses two or more colors to divide squares into triangles, and two rows are arranged so that either the same colors or tones touch. A Chevron border can either be pieced as separate rows or into four-patch blocks and then assembled.

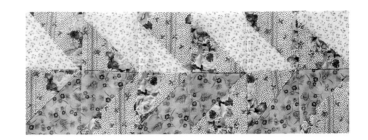

Air Castle

Size of finished patch: 4 in.

This pattern of triangle squares with one half split appears in many quilt blocks. The grain direction is different on the large and small triangles. First, piece identical triangles from the small ones, press seams to the dark side, and then piece the squares and assemble in a row.

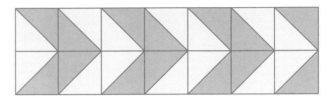

Mitered Stripes

Size of finished border: 6 in. wide

Width of strip: 1–2½ in.

Use the leftovers from the quilt top for this border so that the design of the matching colored border will not clash with the block design. Cut the strips and piece together at random to form a long ribbon. Press all seams in the same direction. Fold and cut one end of the border at a right angle and stitch the length to one edge of the quilt top, starting and ending the seam about ¼ in. from each end. At the uncut end, fold the border at right angles and cut. Piece a second edge in the same way. Bring the two diagonals together and stitch from the quilt to the outside. Open the seam out and press. Repeat on all sides of the quilt.

Nine Patch

Size of finished block: 6 in. square

Patches on this nine-patch block can be worked in many different color combinations, although two is enough. Piece the blocks together to make a border ribbon.

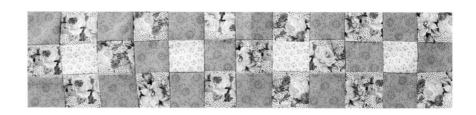

Diamond Squares

Size of finished patch: 4 in. square

Cut the triangles with the grain along a short edge, and the squares with the grain from point to point. Piece the long edge of the triangles to the squares and press seams outward. Join patches to make a border ribbon. Keeping the coloring simple—four colors only—gives the border more impact.

Dog Tooth

Size of finished triangle/border:

4 in. wide

The triangles are equilateral, each angle being 60°, and have the grain running from a point to the center. Piece one triangle to another, press the seam to the darker side, and then piece the next to make a continuous border ribbon.

Dog Tooth Split

Size of finished border: 4 in. wide

First, piece the long edges of the half triangles together to make rectangles, press the seams to the dark side, and then piece the rectangles together to make a continuous border ribbon.

Flying Geese

Size of finished border: 6 in. wide

For the small triangles, the grain runs along the short edge while for the large ones it runs point to base. Piece the long edge of the small triangles to the short edge of the large ones and press the seams toward the small triangles. Repeat on the opposite side and then piece these together, point to base, one after the other to make a continuous border ribbon. Be careful to keep the points intact.

Flying Geese 2

Size of finished border: 6 in. wide

Assemble large and small triangles in two colorways in the same way as for Flying Geese. Piece the Flying Geese base to base to form squares, and then piece these together, one after the other, to make a continuous border ribbon. Be careful to keep the points intact.

Ribbon

Size of finished border: 8 in. wide

This border is made up of two rows of triangle squares pieced above and below a row of squares. Piece the triangle squares and then assemble into rectangles by sandwiching a square of the same color between by each vertical pair. To achieve a concertina effect for the ribbon, use contrasting tones and piece them mirror image. These are then pieced lengthwise to make a continuous strip.

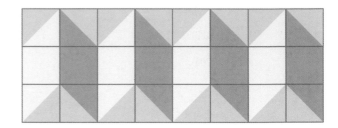

Nelson's Victory

Size of finished border: 4¾ in. wide

Despite its name, this border looks like Beach Huts upside down. Cut differently colored four-sided shapes so that they make mirror images of each other. Piece the triangles to the diagonals of the four-sided shapes and press the seams toward the triangles. Then piece these one after the other to make a continuous border ribbon.

APPLIQUÉ BLOCKS

The appliqué blocks work equally well when stitched by hand or machine, although the finished effect will be very different. Hand-stitching will give a more traditional look with the edges appearing to blend in with the background, while machine-satin stitch outlines the motif. When hand-appliquéing, it's advisable to use plain or patterned fabrics with a small repeat design. If working by machine you can afford to use paler or less distinct fabrics.

Appliqué blocks

Scale the templates on pages 64–96 up or down to the size you require for your block. Cut backing squares larger than required and trim to size and shape once appliquéd and pressed. When cutting out the motifs, keep the line of symmetry to the line of the grain so that there will be the same amount of stretch on each side of the motif if it is slightly distorted with stitching. Stitch clockwise around motifs.

Single Tulip, Tulip Bunch, Butterfly, Dragonfly

Finished block with frame: 10½ in. square

Central appliqué: 7½ in. square

Cut the backing fabric to 10 in. square, make the templates, and cut out the motifs. Pin the motifs in place, keeping them within an area of 7 in. square.

■ **Single Tulip** To start, lay the top thread along the line of stitching and stitch over it for about 1 in. before trimming it off. This will conceal and secure it. Satin stitch (stitch width 3) from the base of a leaf to its tip along the outside edge. With the needle down and on the outside of the motif, turn the fabric and stitch the inner edge of the leaf. Without breaking off, stitch the second leaf and then the straight stem toward the tulip. Draw the threads to the front and tuck them under the tulip, to hide and secure them. (See page 66 for the stitching order when following the instructions).

■ Starting at the center top of the tulip under the pinned petal, stitch up to the right hand point, spin the fabric around the needle again (the needle should always be on the side away from the motif), then stitch around the base and back up and around the other point. Draw threads to the front and tuck behind the petal.

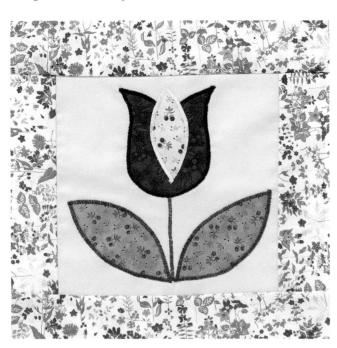

Tulip

Tulip bunch

■ Start stitching the petal midway along one edge, progress to a point, go along the other edge, to a point, and back to where you started. Draw the threads to the back, tie, and trim. Trim the other thread ends on the back.

■ **Tulip Bunch** Work the leaves and one stem as for the Single Tulip. Work the remaining stems next by starting from just under a tulip and stitching toward the base. Turn and stitch back up the final stem. Work the tulips as for the Single Tulip.

■ **Butterfly and Dragonfly** Leave a small space between the wings to avoid a bulge under the body. Work the wings first. For the body, start on one antenna (reduce stitch width to 2) and stitch about ½ in. toward the body. Stop, lift the needle, and pull back to stitch the second antenna (don't break off the thread). Increase the stitch width to 3 and stitch the body. Draw threads to the back, tic, and trim.

Butterflies

Dragonflies

■ Press the appliquéd block on the wrong side and trim it to 8½ in.

■ Cut 2½-in. strips of fabric for the frame. Taking a ½-in. seam allowance, sew on the side strips first, then the top and bottom. (Each block will need a strip 40 in. long.) Press seams outwards, away from the center square.

Leaf Ring and Bird and Bee blocks with Multi fabric frames

Finished block with frame: 13 in. square

Central appliqué: 10 in. square

Cut the backing fabric to 11½ in. square, make templates, and cut out the motifs. Keep the line of symmetry to the line of the grain, especially on the bird. Pin the motifs in place, keeping them within an area of 9 in.

■ **Leaf Ring** Draw a 3 in. radius circle with a quilter's pencil on the backing fabric. Cut out 16 small leaves, a daisy, and a 1¼-in. circle—no need for a template, just draw around a coin—in as many different fabrics as you wish.

■ Stitch the leaves, changing the thread to tone each time. Start stitching near the ring and stitch over the top thread to conceal it when you start. Draw threads to the back and trim as each leaf is finished. When you stitch the ring, all these threads will be secured as you stitch over the tips of the leaves. Tie the threads at the back when the patch is finished.

■ **Bird and Bee** Draw a short section of a 3 in. radius circle for the stem.

■ Stitch the bird's beak and legs first, then the body, starting and ending just under the wing, which will hide threads pulled to the front. The eye is a ¼ in. line of stitching on the widest setting. Tie threads at the back and trim.

■ Stitch the leaves in pairs and change the thread for the stem. The bud conceals the ends of the stem threads.

■ The bee wings should just touch, but not overlap, to avoid a bulge under the body. Two horizontal lines of brown stitching represent its markings.

Sewing order

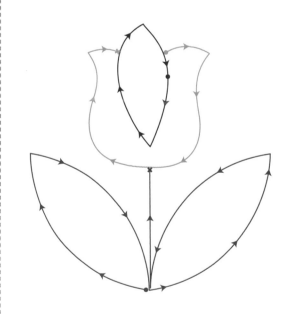

——— First

——— Second

——— Third

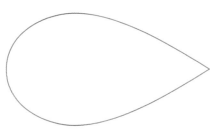

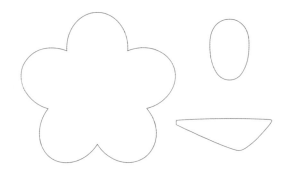

■ Press the block on the wrong side and trim it to 10½ in. square.

■ Cut frame strips 2½ in. wide and in varied lengths of 4–6¼ in. Stitch together at random. You will need a length of about 51 in. for each block. Taking a ½-in. seam allowance, sew a strip to each side and then to the top and bottom. Press seams outward, away from the center square.

Leaf Ring

Bird and Bee

Hearts, Dove, Tulips, and Flower

Hearts, doves, and tulips are traditional quilt block themes and are here worked by hand in red-and-white gingham and plain red, reminiscent of the "Turkey red" of vintage quilts. The motifs are shown on table linen and a pillowcase (see pages 138–139 and 145) but would also work well on a sampler quilt, where you could vary the direction of the dove and the number of tulips, and experiment with a different placement of hearts on each block.

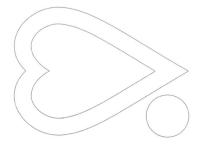

Size of finished block: 9½ in. square

■ Cut the backing fabric 13 in. square.

■ As all these motifs are fairly small, you do not need to match the direction of grain on the motif to that of the backing fabric, but you do need to keep the line of symmetry to the line of grain. Add ¼ in. extra around each template for turning under.

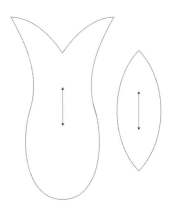

■ The diagrams show which layer to stitch first and the best starting point. Use threads in colors that match the darkest of the appliqué fabrics. You will need to snip into the sharp curves in the turn-under allowance at the top of the hearts. Leave the detail stitching of stems and bird eye until last and use three strands of embroidery floss and running stitch.

■ If you are stitching by machine, use stitch width 3, narrowing to 1 for the detailing.

Heart

Dove

Tulips

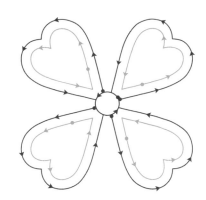

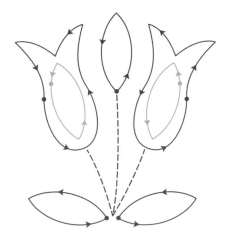

First
Second
Third

First
Second
Third

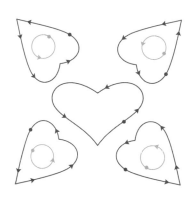

First
Second
Third

First
Second

Flower

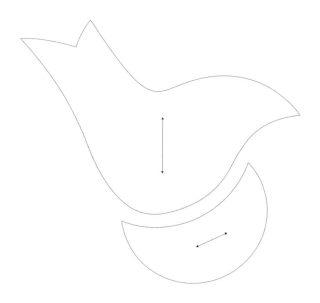

Leaf motifs

The ash, maple and oak motifs are used together on a pillow (page 144). Alternatively, you could work each block in a different color, to indicate different seasons, and use them on a quilt top or hanging. The holly design could be applied to Christmas tablecloths, napkins, or stockings, or three leaves could be reduced in size for cards with beads or buttons for the berries.

Ash and holly width: 9 in. square

Maple and oak width: 12 in. square

Satin stitch width: 3, narrowing to 1 for detailing

■ Cut the backing fabric 1½ in. larger than required. You can trim it to size later.

■ Cut the motifs with the grain line running along the length of the leaf; this gives equal stretch around the motif and makes it less likely to stretch.

■ Draw the branches in chalk and then pin the leaves either side. Start stitching the leaves near the branches, as the branch satin stitching will conceal the thread ends. If you are working by hand, use stem stitch for the branches and running stitch for the veins.

Ash

■ As the ash keys are on top of the leaves, stitch these after you have appliquéd the leaves.

Holly

■ Leave the detail stitching of the veins on the holly and the branch until last. For the veins, work toward the branch, widening the satin stitch as you proceed.

Maple and oak

■ The maple and oak veins are best worked from a narrow to a wide satin stitch, with the central vein concealing all the other stitch endings and widening to form the branch.

Ash

Holly

Maple

Oak

Flowers in bunches

Use several different fabrics on the flower heads and change the thread color to give variety.

Size of finished block: 8 x 11 in.

Satin stitch width: 3, narrowing to 1 on the points

■ For these two flowers, first stitch the stems, and then appliqué the flower heads and leaves.

■ If you are working by hand, work the stems in stem or running stitch. As the motifs are small, pin and turn the allowance under with the point of the needle as you slipstitch. On the bluebells, you will need to snip into the sharp angles.

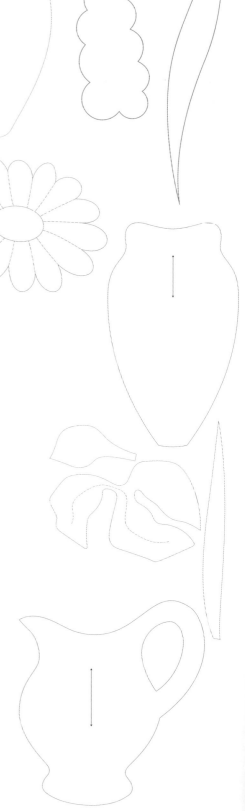

Bluebells   *Hyacinth*

Flowers in vases

Highly patterned printed lawns are good here, with bold repeating designs on the vases, floral designs on the flower heads and leaves, and plain fabrics for the flower centers. Try to center the vases so that they look symmetrical.

Cornflower: 13 x 21 in.

Daisy: 13 x 20 in.

Iris: 13 x 22 in.

Satin stitch width: 3, narrowing to 1 for detailing

■ Pin the motifs in place and draw the stems lightly in chalk.

■ First stitch the stems from vase to flower head. The start and finish of the stitching will then be concealed under the appliqué motifs. Use stitch width 3 if you are machine stitching, and stem stitch with embroidery floss if working by hand.

■ Then stitch on the flower heads. If you are working by machine, start on an inside curve where it will show least; if working by hand, start on a smooth curve.

■ Stitch the daisy heads as if the petals were separate pieces, starting narrow (width 1) and widening the stitch to 3 as you go from just under the center and around the petal tips. Stop and lift the needle and presser foot without breaking the thread and start from the center again on the next petal, stitching over the loop of thread.

■ On the irises, stitch the pale petal first and then the three darker petals. Do the detailing last, starting narrow and widening the stitch toward the center of the flower.

■ The cornflower has tight curves, so lift the presser foot with the needle still in the fabric of the motif and turn the panel around the needle.

■ Next, appliqué the flower centers.

■ Finally, appliqué the jug or vase. Stitch the inside of the jug and urn handles first, and then the outside edges.

Daisy in vase

Iris in a vase

Cornflower vase

Appliqué Rooster and Hen

The rooster is used on a wall-hanging project with a patchwork border (see page 133), but it would work equally well as the central panel on a pillow. These designs have several layers, which can put strain and distort the backing fabric, so use calico or a sturdy furnishing linen as the backing.

Size of finished block: 16 in. square

Motif height: 14 in. square

Satin stitch width: 3, narrowing to 1 at the points

■ Cut the backing about 10 percent larger than required and trim it to shape and size when the piece has been stitched and pressed. Use threads that match the darkest or brightest color in the fabrics to make the design more vibrant.

■ Cut all the pieces on the straight of grain, with the larger pieces matching the grain line of the backing fabric to avoid distortion.

■ Pin all the pieces in place, one layer on another. The layers should all overlap a little.

■ The stitching diagram shows the order in which to work. The start and finish of many layers is concealed under an upper layer.

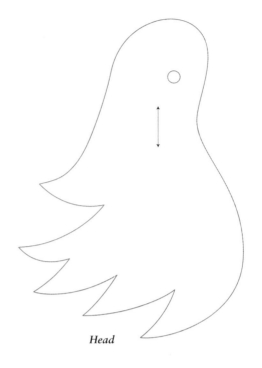

Head

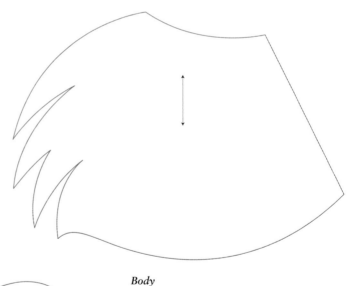

Body

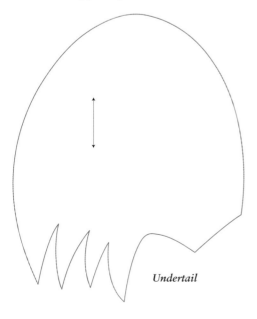

Undertail

Tail feathers

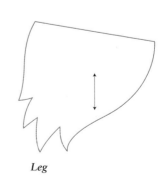

Leg

Rooster

■ For the rooster, first stitch the feet, comb, and undertail, starting and finishing just under the overlapping layers and narrowing the stitch width as you approach the points.

■ Work the leg and then the body. Next, stitch the upper tail feathers, starting near the body. Then stitch the ruff, throat, and beak, starting the beak nearest the eye.

■ Finally work the eye, on stitch width 3 or 4. Work a couple of stitches, stop with the needle in the fabric, spin the fabric a fraction and work another couple of stitches; continue until you have completed a circle.

Feet, comb, beak, throat

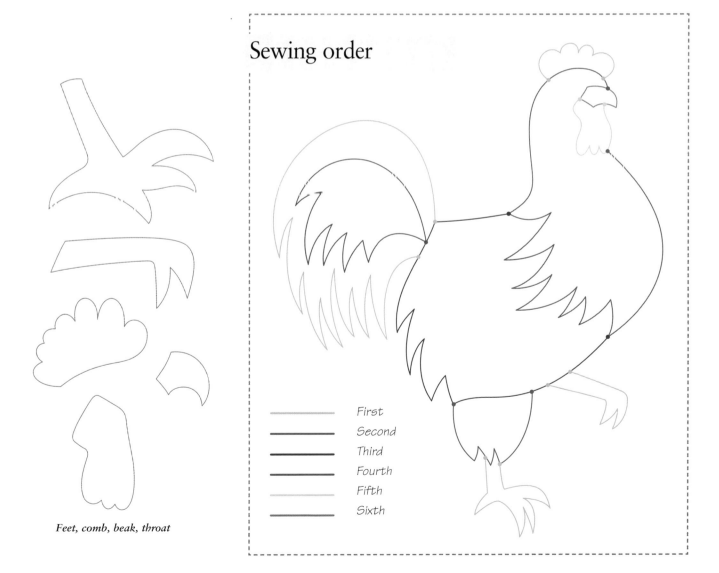

Sewing order

———	First
———	Second
———	Third
———	Fourth
———	Fifth
———	Sixth

Hen

■ For the hen, first stitch the feet, comb, and tail feathers, then the tail and body. Next stitch the upper wing and then the wing feather. Finally, stitch the ruff, throat and beak, and eye.

■ Bring the threads of both blocks to the back of the fabric, tie, and trim.

■ Press on the wrong side and trim the blocks to shape and size.

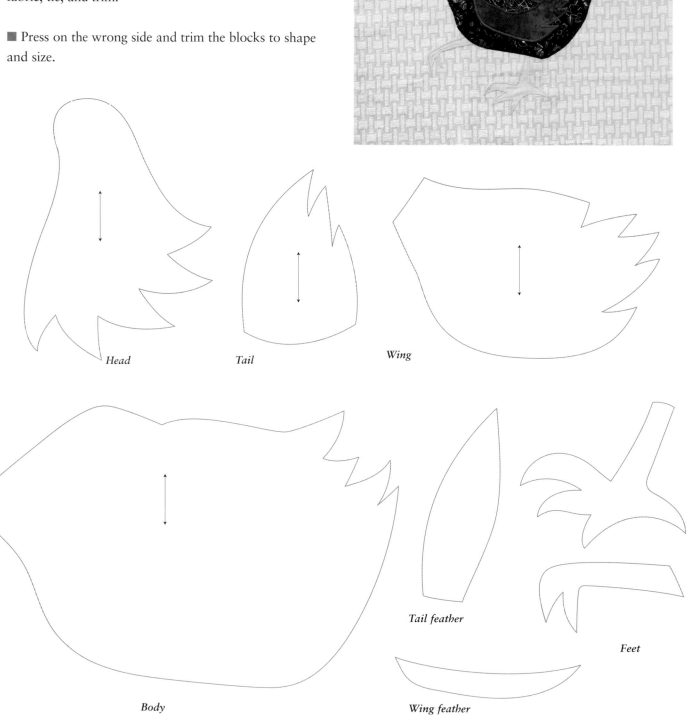

Head

Tail

Wing

Tail feather

Feet

Body

Wing feather

Comb, beak, and throat

Sewing order

————	*First*
————	*Second*
————	*Third*
————	*Fourth*
————	*Fifth*
————	*Sixth*
————	*Seventh*
————	*Eighth*

Sleeping Cat

This block, with its simple, smooth outline and intricate detailing on the face, can be worked either by hand or machine. Use as the center panel on a pillow or stitch cat blocks in different fabrics together to make a quilt.

Size of finished block: 12 in. square

Satin stitch width: 3, narrowing to 1 for detailing

■ The motif is large and liable to stretch out of shape, so cut it with the grain line running vertically and match to the grain of the backing fabric. Take care when pinning the cat in place on the backing fabric, as the legs and tail may distort.

■ Start stitching on the back leg that is farthest away, work around it and onto the belly, toward the front legs and so on. When you have finished, carry on stitching across the top of the first leg and onto the body a little way to detail the thigh.

■ Work the face detail stitching last, setting a very narrow stitch width for the whiskers and eyes and a slightly wider one for the mouth. The nose is a triangle worked in width 2 satin stitch and then filled in with more rows of satin stitch. If you are hand stitching, use stem stitch for the eyes and mouth, satin stitch for the nose, and running stitch for the whiskers.

Farmyard motifs

These motifs are used on a child's crib quilt (see page 132), but could also be made into colorful wall hangings for a bedroom or playroom.

Size of finished blocks: 12 in. square

Satin stitch width: 3, narrowing to 1 for detailing

■ Many of these motifs are layered. The diagrams show the order in which to appliqué them to the background fabric. If you are working by machine, start stitching on an inside corner where it will show least, bring threads to the back, tie, and trim. If you are working by hand, start on a smooth curve or straight area.

Pigs

■ Stitch the legs that are farthest away first, and then the rest of the pigs. Narrow the stitch to width 1 for the snout and tail details. It is easiest to stitch the tail from the tip. Leave the needle in the fabric, lift the presser foot, and turn a little every few stitches to work the curl. If hand stitching, use chain stitch for the tail.

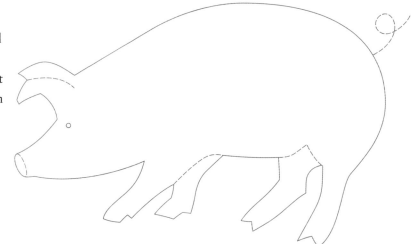

Sewing order

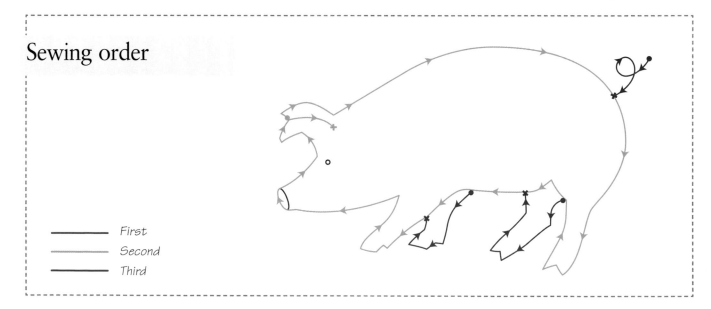

———— First

———— Second

———— Third

Tractor

■ First stitch the hay bales, then the cart and tractor, leaving the wheels until last.

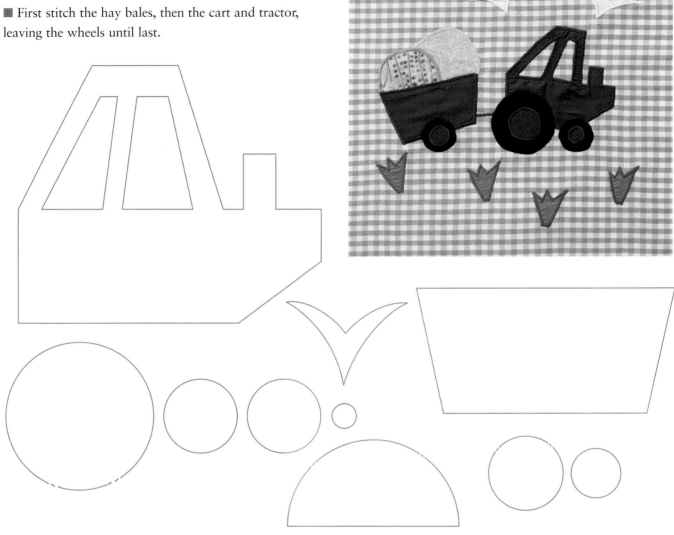

Sewing order

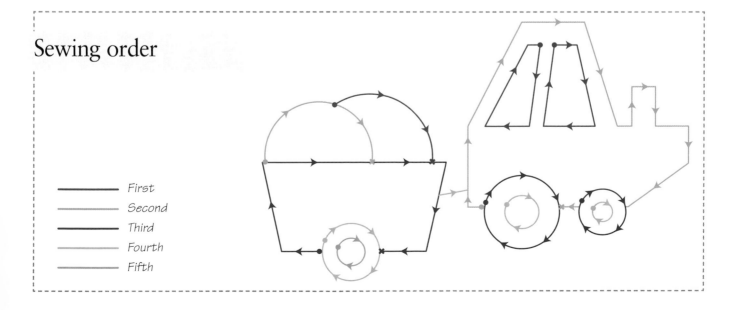

First
Second
Third
Fourth
Fifth

Sheep

■ Stitch the legs first (the body will conceal the stop and start of the stitching), then the bodies, and finally the heads.

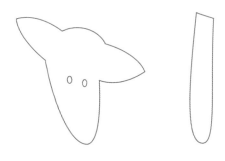

Sewing order

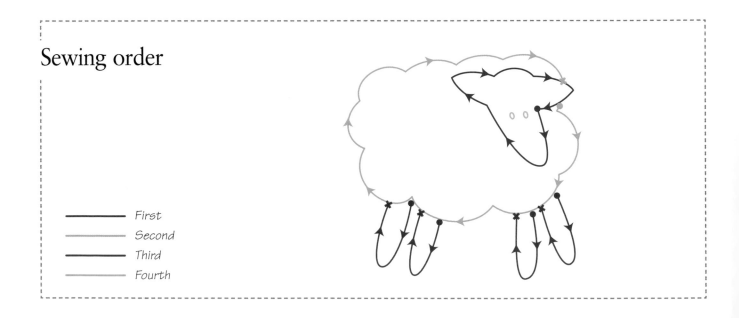

——— First
——— Second
——— Third
——— Fourth

Cows

■ Stitch the udders and then the legs that are farthest away first, before the rest of the cow bodies. Stitch the white patches and then the detailing. Note that the eyes are not round but tiny crescent shapes.

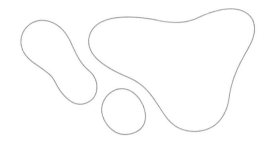

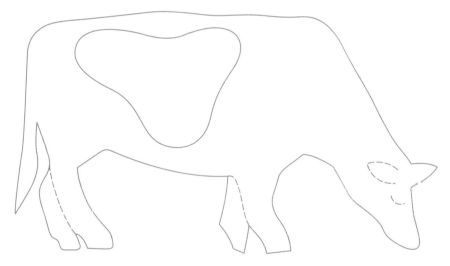

Sewing order

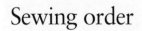

First
Second
Third

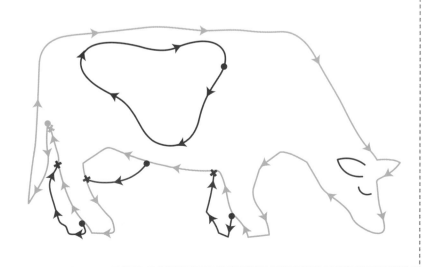

Christmas motifs

These motifs are used on Christmas cards but could also be appliquéd to Christmas stockings or sacks, table napkins, and tablecloths. Add extra branches to make a taller tree.

Size of finished block: 9 in. square

Satin stitch width: 3, and 1 for detailing

Trees

■ Stitch the trunks first, so that the thread ends are concealed under the foliage, and if machine stitching, reduce the stitch width on the branches.

Snowman

■ Stitch the balls of snow first, starting with the lower one. Begin stitching just under the overlap of the smaller ball of snow to conceal the thread ends. Next, stitch the scarf and hat. Leave the detailing until last and stitch from the pointed ends to the wide, widening the stitch as you work. The eyes and buttons are in stitch width 2, working 12 stitches very close together.

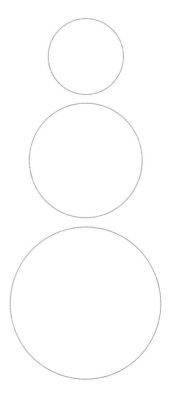

Watery motifs

The fish motifs are used on the Children's Counting Quilt (see page 130), as well as on the Album Cover (see page 129). The designs on this page and on pages 84 and 85 could also be used on curtains, duvet covers, children's pockets, overall bibs, or beach bags.

Size of finished block: 9½ in. square

Satin stitch width: 3, narrowing to 1 for detailing

■ Cut the motifs with the grain line running vertically; this gives equal stretch around the motif and makes the fabric less likely to distort. Cut the backing fabric larger than required—say 12 in. square—and trim it to size later. When you pin the motifs in place, remember to keep them well within a 9-in. central window.

■ Start stitching on an inside corner where the stitching will show least. When you have finished, bring the threads to the back, tie, and trim.

■ Always leave detail stitching and the fishes' eyes until last and use a darker color of thread.

Tips

● Narrow the stitch width on the spikes of the spiky fish, the palm, and the gulls to make them more pointed.

● The eyes of the slender fish, fat fish, fancy fish, and the seahorse are made of about six satin stitches very close together, with threads tied and trimmed at the back.

● Pin the seahorse well or it will be likely to distort as you stitch.

● Widen the stitch width as you sew the shell and starfish details. I find it easier to start narrow and end wide; the detail stitching on the starfish ends at its center.

● Match the grain line of the sun and island to the backing fabric to avoid rippling. Appliqué these pieces first, then stitch the trunk, and finally the leaves. Start stitching the trunk, from the top, so that the start and finish are concealed by the leaves.

Spiky and slender fish

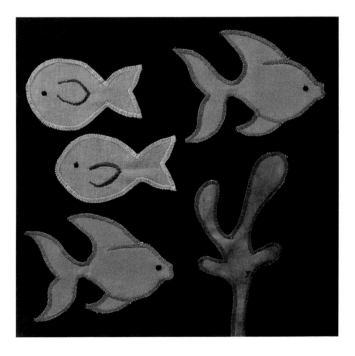

Fat and fancy fishes

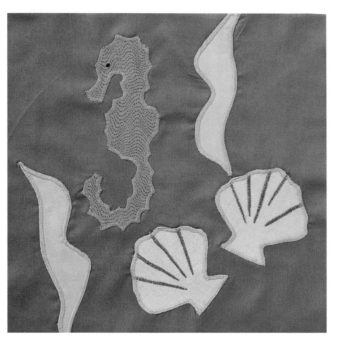

Seahorse and shells

Green fish and starfish

Palm tree island

Sailing boat

Fruit bowls

These blocks have been hand stitched, but you could make them just as well by machine. The blocks could be used as pillow panels. If joined with sashing across a wall hanging or quilt, they would be reminiscent of traditional Baltimore designs, with every block having a different set of fruit and placements.

Size of finished blocks: 14½ in. square

Satin stitch width: 3, narrowing to 1 for detailing

■ The diagrams show which pieces to stitch first, working up from layer to layer; always start stitching just under an overlap. You will need to snip into the turning allowance on inside curves, such as the foot of the bowl and the pineapple leaves, to achieve a smooth curve. Leave the detail stitching to last. If you are working by machine, use stitch width 3, narrowing to 1 on the pineapple leaf tips and all the detailing.

■ The oranges and lemons are slightly padded with batting, giving a raised effect. The batting is poked under the fruit through a gap in the stitching when the stitching is almost complete.

■ For detailing, the oranges and lemons have cross-stitches, the grapes stem stitches, and the cherries chain stitches; the apple and pear stalks are satin stitched.

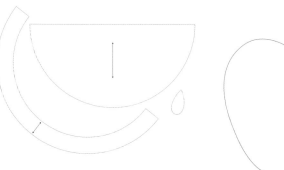

Bowl with pineapple and watermelon slice

Basket with apples and pears

Basket with grapes and strawberries

Sewing orders

First
Second
Third

First
Second
Third
Fourth
Fifth

First
Second
Third

First
Second
Third

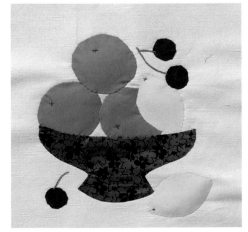

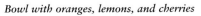

Bowl with oranges, lemons, and cherries

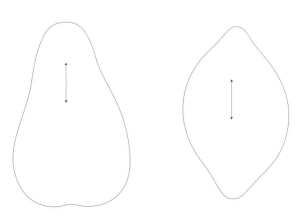

Hawaiian appliqué

Hawaiian motifs are very often worked in dark colors on a white background, although a patterned background fabric can make the quilt a little less stark. Use different motifs for each block.

Size of finished block: 14 in. square

Size of motif: 10 in.

■ To make the template, take a piece of paper the size you want the motif to be and fold it in quarters and then diagonally. Draw a spiky snowflake design radiating from the center, cut through all the layers, and unfold— much like a child's paper-people chain.

■ Pin the template to the motif fabric, making sure the grain is vertical, add a turning allowance of maximum ¼ in.—narrower is better if the design is spindly—and cut.

■ Baste the motif to the backing fabric along the spindles and start stitching on a straight area. If you have a cut-out in the center of the motif, work this last. Press from on the wrong side.

Orange Peel

This is traditionally worked in just two colors, as in the project (page 154). You could also vary the color of the backing squares diagonally with white segments throughout. This block is best pieced by hand.

Size of finished block: 11 in. square

■ For the template, draw a 5½ in. square. Placing the compass point in one corner, trace a quarter circle with a 5½ in. radius. Repeat from the opposite corner. Cut out the resulting segment shape.

■ Pin the template to the motif fabric, with the grain running along the length of the shape. Add a ¼ in. turning allowance and cut out.

■ The backing fabric is best cut 6½ in. square and trimmed to size once appliquéd. Fold the square diagonally and use the crease line as a positioning guide for the segment. Hand appliqué the motifs in place.

■ Piece patches into vertical pairs and then assemble these strips to make the blocks.

Appliqué alphabet

These monograms can be used on many items, such as personalized pillows, scarves, and pockets. They could even be worked intertwined on an appliqué wedding quilt block. The motifs are large and liable to stretch out of shape, so always cut with the grain line running vertically and match to the grain of the backing fabric.

Size of finished block: 9½ in. square

Motif height: 6½ in.

Satin stitch width: 3

■ Cut the backing fabric about 10 percent larger than required. It will be trimmed to size once it has been stitched and pressed.

■ Pin the motifs carefully to the backing fabric—say, eight pins per motif—with the pins going across so that you can remove them easily as you machine stitch.

■ Some letters, such as M, V, and S, are simple, with no cross-over stitching. By machine, start stitching these letters at an inside corner, where the stitching will show least. For the other letters, the diagrams (see pages 92–93) show the easiest direction in which to stitch, with the least number of threads to tie off at the beginning and end. The start and finish of the first line of stitching will be concealed by the subsequent stitch lines.

■ If you are hand stitching, start on a straight or smooth curve, not an inside corner, and work counterclockwise, using slipstitch. On the letters that have cross-overs (A, C, D, for example), hand embroider along the cross-over lines in stem, running, or chain stitch using embroidery floss.

■ The stitch directions on the diagrams are for machine stitching, which is best worked with the motif to the left of the needle, whereas hand stitching should be worked counterclockwise.

Templates

D E F G

L M N

R S T

Templates

Sewing order

●	Start
✗	Finish
——	First
——	Second
——	Third

Appliqué numbers

These numbers are used on the Child's Counting Quilt on page 130. You could also appliqué them onto children's pockets, bags, or overall bibs, or scatter them on a plain curtain or duvet cover. Reduced to quarter size, they could be used on "age" birthday cards.

Size of finished block: 4¼ in.

Motifs: 3½ in. tall

Satin stitch width: 3

■ Cut the motifs with the grain line running vertically. If you enlarge the numbers, it is best to match the grain of the motif to the grain of the backing fabric to avoid the risk of distortion and rippling.

■ The numbers 1, 2, 3, 5, and 7 can be stitched in one continuous line. If you are machine stitching, start stitching at an inside corner, where the stitching will show the least. To maneuver around sharp corners, keep the needle in the fabric on the side of stitching away from the motif and spin the fabric around the needle before continuing.

■ On the numbers 4, 6, 8, 9, and 0, stitch the center rings first and then work the outside of the motif, starting at an inside corner whenever possible.

■ If you are hand stitching, start on a straight or smooth curved area and work counterclockwise. Stitch the center rings first.

Templates

0 1 2 3 4 5 6 7 8 9

PROJECTS

Substitute any of the blocks used on the projects to make a
pillow, bag, or quilt personal to you. The quantities given for each
project in the "You will need" boxes are based on fabrics at least
45 in. wide. "Fat quarters" are great for appliqué, but avoid them
when buying material for patchwork projects as you will be working
with full-width fabric.

Four Patch silk scarf

The simple Four Patch block looks vibrant and jewel-like when isolated with plain borders. Silk is easy to sew because it holds a crease so well. This scarf has eight Four Patch windows, each measuring just 2½ in. square. As silk can fray easily, the seam allowances are all ½ in.

Size of scarf: 11 x 65 in.
Size of finished block: 2½ in. square

■ Cut a strip along the length of the fabric 12 in. wide x 66 in. long for the backing, and two strips 5 in. wide x 66 in. long for the sides of the scarf. From the remaining fabric, cut nine 3½ x 6 in. strips for the sashing between the blocks.

■ Referring to the Four Patch block (see page 10), draft and make eight multicolored blocks with bright silk squares, taking a ½-in. seam allowance throughout.

■ Stitch the blocks together alternating with short strips of black silk to make the central band, with a strip of black at each end. Press the seams toward the black fabric.

■ Stitch the side strips to the patchwork panel and press the seams toward the side strips.

■ Lay the scarf on the backing fabric, with right sides together, and pin it in place. Silk frays easily, so use a small stitch. Machine stitch all around, leaving a gap of 4 in. near the center of one long edge. Trim the corners and turn right side out. Hand stitch the gap closed and press.

You will need

- 2 yd black silk
- 32 squares of bright silks, each 2¼ x 2¼ in.
- Matching thread

Courthouse Steps silk purse

Foundation blocks are easy to piece on a small scale—and the foundation fabric gives a slight stiffness to the work. This little purse is made up of three Courthouse Steps blocks—one each for the front, back, and flap—and has a red silk lining. The vibrant scraps of silk catch and reflect the light, making it perfect for an evening purse.

Size of purse: 3½ in. square
Size of finished block: 3½ in. square

■ Referring to the Courthouse Steps block (see pages 54–55), draft and make three blocks as shown, using 1-in. silk strips and a ¼-in. seam allowance throughout. The blocks should each be 3½ in. square, plus the seam allowance.

■ Trim away the excess foundation fabric and then sew the blocks together in a strip. Trim the lining to the same size as the patchwork. With right sides together, stitch the patchwork to the lining, leaving a 2-in. gap in one side. Trim the corners and turn right side out. Hand stitch the gap closed and press.

■ Fold the purse in thirds and hand stitch the two sides together. If desired, sew on a snap to secure the flap.

You will need

- Silk scraps in seven colors, cut 1 in. wide and a maximum of 24 in. long
- Three 4½-in. foundation squares
- 4½- x 12½-in. piece of lining fabric in a color to match the center square
- Matching thread

Child's apron with patchwork pockets

Make the apron from sturdy, washable calico or fine canvas so that it's suitable for cooking, painting, craft, and other messy activities. Three sizes are given—two for children and one adult size. For the blocks, I used plain, bright fabrics that stand out from the apron and chose Fly, Big Dipper, and Broken Dishes for the pockets (see pages 11, 12, and 13). Any border strip would also work well, but complex blocks could look fussy on the big check of the apron fabric.

■ From the calico or canvas, cut a rectangle 21 x 27, 27 x 33, or 35 x 43 in. and cut away two quarter circles with a radius of 5, 7, or 13¾ in. at the top corners.

Sizes of apron: 17 x 23 in., 23 x 29 in., or 31 x 39 in.
Size of finished block: 6 in. square

You will need

- 27½, 33½, or 43¼ in. calico or canvas
- Scraps of red, blue, pale green, and dark green for pockets, each 4 x 16 in.
- Large snap
- Matching thread

■ Also from the length of the calico or canvas, cut two 17- x 3-in. waist strips, and a 17- x 2½-in. neck strip. Fold all three strips in half lengthwise, turn in raw edges, and topstitch, folding under one short end also. Cut a 18½- x 7-in. piece of canvas or calico for the pocket lining.

■ Fold over 1 in. twice around the edge of the apron and topstitch.

■ Referring to the patchwork blocks, draft and piece three blocks—each 6-in. square, plus the seam allowance.

■ Sew the blocks together edge to edge and press the seams in the same direction along the strip. With right sides together, stitch the blocks to the lining along the top edge and press the seam away from blocks. Fold in half, so that the lower edges of the blocks and the lining are level, and ½ in. of lining folded over along the top edge. Stitch all the way around, leaving an 3-in. gap in one edge. Turn right side out, press flat, and topstitch the top edge; then pin and stitch to the apron.

Stitch between the blocks to make compartments in the pocket strip.

■ Lay the apron wrong side up, pin the unfinished ends of the waist straps just below the arm curve, and the neck strap to the top edges of bib top (left of bib only for a child) so that they point toward the apron, and stitch along the turning seams. Turn the apron over and topstitch the straps close to the edges to secure.

■ Stitch the snap to the inside of the top right side of the bib and to the neck strap end for a child's apron. If you are making an adult-sized apron, the neck strap can be stitched to the bib at both ends.

Patchwork bookmarks

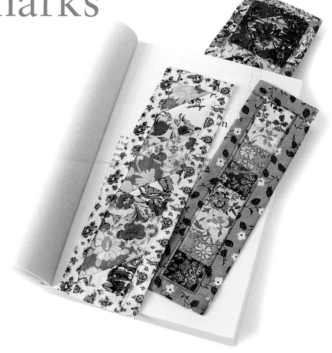

Choose simple border blocks that are one patch deep or foundation blocks when working on a small scale. The foundation backings help to keep tiny blocks square. The designs are based on Sawtooth, Diamond Squares, and Squares borders, with the backing of the bookmarks folded over to the front as the binding. The borders vary from ½–⅝ in. wide.

Size of bookmark: 2½ x 8½ in.

■ For Sawtooth, draft and make five 1⅜-in. triangle squares in random colors and piece edge to edge into a strip (see page 28). For Diamond Squares, draft and

make four finished size 2-in. blocks and piece edge to edge into a strip (see page 58). For Squares, cut and piece eight finished size 1-in. squares into a strip. Press the seams in the same direction along the strips.

■ Center the patchwork on the backing fabric, with the interlining sandwiched in between, and pin the three layers together. Fold the top and bottom edges of the backing fabric to the front, folding under the raw edges, and topstitch. Repeat at the sides and press.

You will need

- Scraps of fabric for the patchwork
- 2½- x 8½-in. piece of cotton for the interlining
- 4- x 10-in. piece of fabric for backing
- Matching thread

Six-Point Christmas Star

Each of the diamonds is in a different pattern, so making this star is a good way of using up scraps of Christmas designs, ginghams, stripes, and other small-patterned fabrics to match your Christmas decor. You could also use velvets, silks, and sparkly fabrics.

Size of star: 8½ in. across
Length of finished diamond: 4¼ in.

■ Referring to the Six-Pointed Star block (see page 42), draft and cut 12 diamonds in different fabrics—each 4¼ in. long, plus the seam allowance. Piece into two six-point stars—but press all the seams open, not to the side, to avoid puckering at the seams when you pad it.

■ Place the two stars right sides together and stitch around the edge, leaving a gap on one of the seams midway between a point and a seam. Turn right side out, pad with batting, and hand stitch the gap closed.

■ To hang the star, stitch a short length of gold thread through one of the points and knot the ends.

You will need

- Small scraps of 12 harmonizing fabrics
- Scraps of batting or toy stuffing
- Matching thread
- Gold thread to hang

Crazy Christmas stocking

Use up all those leftover snippets of Christmas fabric for this stocking. It has a solid fabric cuff and back, but you could crazy-patch both sides.

Size of stocking: 17 in. tall x 8 in. wide at top

■ Make your template and cut the foundation fabric about 2 in. larger than required. Referring to the Crazy Patchwork block on page 163, work the front of the stocking. Press and trim to shape, 17½ in. tall x 8½ in. wide at the top. Cut the back of the stocking, remembering to turn the template over.

■ With right sides together, stitch the front and back of the stocking together. With right sides together, sew the two strips for the cuff into a ring and hem one long side of the cuff. Slide the cuff over the top of the stocking, with the folded loop sandwiched in between, and stitch around the top. Turn the stocking right side out, fold the cuff down, and press.

You will need

- 18- x 13-in. piece of foundation fabric (double if you are crazy patching both sides)
- Scraps of Christmas fabric for the patchwork
- Two 8½- x 3½-in. strips for the cuff
- 18- x 13-in. piece of fabric for the back (unless you are crazy patching both sides)
- 8½- x 1½-in. strip folded and topstitched for the hanging loop
- Matching thread

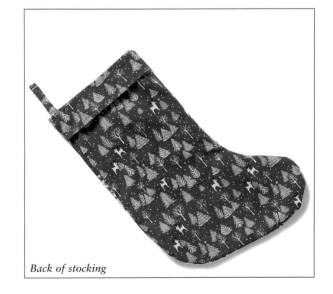

Back of stocking

Sawtooth border napkins

These elegant linen napkins have a random Sawtooth border along two sides and a binding all around the outer edge. You could use any of the border blocks on pages 58–62 for the borders.

Size of napkin: 22 in. square
Width of finished border: 2 in.

■ Referring to the Sawtooth border (see page 58), draft and make 19 triangle squares in random colors—each 2 in. square, plus the seam allowances. Sew them together edge to edge into strips of nine and ten. Press the seams in the same direction along the strips.

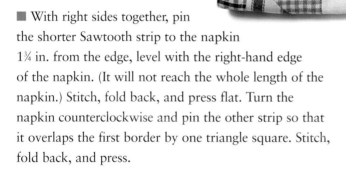

■ With right sides together, pin the shorter Sawtooth strip to the napkin 1¾ in. from the edge, level with the right-hand edge of the napkin. (It will not reach the whole length of the napkin.) Stitch, fold back, and press flat. Turn the napkin counterclockwise and pin the other strip so that it overlaps the first border by one triangle square. Stitch, fold back, and press.

■ Stitch the right side of binding to the back of the napkin, fold the binding over to the front, fold the raw edge under, and topstitch. Working counterclockwise, repeat on all sides, folding in the end of the binding strips and stitching across or hand stitching to neaten.

You will need

- 19 scraps at least 3 in. square for the patchwork
- 22-in. square of linen
- Four 23½- x 1½-in. strips of fabric for the binding
- Matching thread

Diamond Squares napkin rings

The diamond squares on this napkin ring are just 2 in. square. Look for small-patterned fabrics with motifs, such as the blue and red birds, to use as centers, like tiny framed pictures. The backing fabric is folded to the front as binding.

Size of napkin rings: 3 x 7 in.
Size of finished block: 2 in. square

■ Referring to the Diamond Squares border (see page 60), draft and make three diamond squares in two different colors—each 2 in. square, plus the seam allowance—and piece into a strip.

■ Center the patchwork on the backing fabric and pin it in place, sandwiching a layer of fabric or interfacing in between the patchwork and the backing to stiffen. Fold the top and bottom edges of the backing fabric to the front, folding under the raw edges, and topstitch. Repeat at the sides. With right sides together, whipstitch the ends of the ring together and turn it right side out.

You will need

- Scraps of fabric in two colors and three center motifs
- 4¾- x 8¾-in. piece of backing fabric
- 3- x 7-in. piece of interfacing or scrap of cotton fabric
- Matching thread

Gentleman's Fancy shoulder bag

The green in the patchwork panel matches the plain green of the bag's back. Blocks with a central square and radiating patches work best; Air Castle or Pin Wheel are good alternatives.

Size of bag: 18½ x 19½ in.
Size of finished block: 12 in.

■ Referring to the Gentleman's Fancy block (see page 34), draft and make a block 12-in. square, plus the seam allowance.

■ Cut the borders from pink striped fabric. You need two 13- x 5-in. strips for the top and bottom borders cut from the length of the fabric and two 24- x 4-in. strips for the side borders cut from the width. Stitch the top and bottom borders to the block first, and then the side borders. Press the seams outward.

■ Lay the front of the bag on the wadding, tack in place and quilt along all the seams.

■ Cut a 19¼- x 21½-in. piece of green fabric for the back of the bag. Stitch the front of the bag to the back along the lower edge.

■ Cut a 40- x 3-in. strip of pink striped fabric for the strap. Fold it in half, turn under the raw edges and topstitch the strap lengthwise, padding it with scraps of batting as you proceed.

■ With right sides together, stitch the lining to the bag along the top edges, taking a ½-in. seam allowance, sandwiching the strap ends in between the lining and the back about 1 in. in from the sides.

■ Stitch the side seams (lining to lining and front to back), taking a ½ in. seam allowance, leaving a 9½-in. gap in the lining; this will be stitched once the bag has been turned right side out. Pinch the bottom corners together so that the side and bottom seams are in line and stitch across about 1½ in. in from the corners.

■ Turn the bag right side out and push the lining into the bag by 1 in. Topstitch around the top of the bag ½ in. and 2 in. down to create a channel. Snip the seam of this channel on one side of the bag, so you can thread through the elastic, and hand stitch to secure.

You will need

- *17 in. pink striped furnishing-weight fabric for the borders, strap, and patchwork*
- *24 in. green furnishing-weight fabric for the back of bag and patchwork*
- *6- x 35½-in. piece of cream floral furnishing-weight fabric for the patchwork*
- *19- x 40-in. piece of lining fabric*
- *19½-in. square of 2-oz polyester batting*
- *24-in. length of elastic, ¼ in. wide*
- *Matching thread*

Grandmother's Flower Garden pillow

This pillow is made in furnishing fabrics with appliquéd Flower Garden rosettes. It is a good way of using up any leftover rosettes from a quilt project or for trying out the technique.

Size of pillow: 15 in. square

■ Referring to the Grandmother's Flower Garden block (see page 40), draft and make two floral hexagon rosettes, and baste and press five pointed pentagons over papers for the leaves. Press the rosettes and leaves and remove the papers.

■ Cut a 16-in. square of checked fabric for the pillow front. For the back, cut one piece measuring 16 x 12 in. and another measuring 16 x 5 in.

■ Pin and then hand appliqué (using slipstitch) the rosettes and the green leaf shapes to the pillow front.

You will need

- 16 in. checked fabric for the pillow front and back
- 65 in. filling cord
- 20 in. fabric for cording cover
- 8- x 16-in. piece of floral fabric for the rosettes and scraps for the centers and leaves
- 12-in. zipper
- Matching thread
- 15-in. square pillow form

■ Cut the cording fabric on the bias into strips 2 in. wide and sew into a continuous length. Fold the strip over the filling and stitch close to the cord with a zipper foot. Pin around the edge of the pillow front and stitch again. Trim the cording to size, leaving ¾ in. fabric at one end. Fold this under to cover the raw edge of the other end where they meet.

■ With right sides together, baste the two back pieces together along one long side, taking a ½-in. seam. Machine stitch from each corner for 1½ in. Press the seam open and lay the zipper right side down on the wrong side of the seam. Baste and machine stitch the zipper in place. Remove the basting.

■ Open the zipper. With right sides together, stitch the front of the pillow to the back, stitching as close to the cord as possible. Trim the edges and zigzag or overlock to secure and neaten. Turn right side out.

Star upon Stars pillow

The star is made of five different cotton lawn fabrics, bordered and backed by heavier-weight furnishing fabrics, which is best for a floor pillow, as it will take more wear. The pillow form is 22 in. square.

Size of cushion: 21 in. square
Size of finished star block: 18½ in. square
Length of finished diamond: 3½ in.

■ Referring to the Star upon Stars block (see page 45), draft and cut the fabrics. The grain line should run along the center of the diamonds.

■ Each row is in a different fabric. Cut eight diamonds for the center (A) and another eight for the tips (E) of the star, 16 diamonds each for the second (B) and fourth (D) rows, and 24 for the third (C) row.

■ Lay the pieces on a design board in sequence. Piece into eight strips each of ABC, BCD, and CDE. Press the seams in alternate directions. Assemble into star points and then into the star.

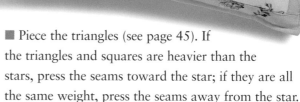

You will need

- 21¾ in. furnishing-weight fabric for the back and borders
- 5 in. lawn fabric in each of four patterns (A, B, D, E)
- 8 in. lawn fabric in fifth pattern (C)
- 10 in. cream floral furnishing-weight fabric for the outer squares and triangles
- 21¾-in. square of 2-oz polyester batting
- 18-in. zipper
- Matching thread
- 22-in. square pillow form

■ Piece the triangles (see page 45). If the triangles and squares are heavier than the stars, press the seams toward the star; if they are all the same weight, press the seams away from the star.

■ From the length of the furnishing fabric, cut four border strips 2 in. wide. Sew the borders first to the side edges (trimming off any excess length), then to the top and bottom. Press the seams toward the borders.

■ Baste the pillow top to the batting. Quilt along the seams around central star A, then around star B, and so on. This will emphasize the starburst effect.

■ Cut one backing piece 22 x 16½ in and another 22 x 6½ in. With right sides facing, baste the two pieces together along one long side, taking a ½-in. seam. Machine stitch from each corner for 1½ in. Press the seam open and lay the zipper right side down on the wrong side of the seam. Baste and then machine stitch the zipper in place. Remove the basting.

■ Pin the patchwork right side down on the pillow back, with zipper open. Machine stitch all around, taking a ½ in. seam allowance, snip off excess fabric on corners and turn cover right side out. Topstitch around the pillow edge.

Swamp Patch floor pillow

When the Swamp Patch blocks are joined edge to edge and two or more fabrics are used for the corner triangles, Broken Dishes blocks appear between the stars. To keep the star pattern prominent, use the darkest fabric on the triangles that make up the arms of each star.

Size of pillow: 29½ in. square
Size of finished block: 13½ in. square

■ From cream floral fabric, cut one back piece measuring 30½ x 22 in. and one measuring 30½ x 8½ in.

■ With right sides together, baste the two back pieces together along one long side taking a ½-in. seam. Machine stitch from each corner for 1½ in. Press the seam open and lay the zipper right side down on the wrong side of the seam. Baste and machine stitch the zipper in place. Remove the basting.

■ From plum fabric, cut four borders measuring 29½ x 2 in. Two of these are slightly longer than needed but it is easier to trim later.

You will need

● 31½ in. large-scale cream floral fabric for the back and center squares
● 14 in. plum fabric for the border and stars
● 6 in. in each of two pink fabrics for the small inner triangles and the corner triangles
● 14 in. cream sprig fabric
● 6 in. of a second cream sprig fabric
● 31½-in. square of 2-oz (70-g) batting
● 27½-in. zipper
● Matching thread
● 31-in. square pillow form

■ Referring to the Swamp Patch block on page 30, draft the templates and cut the pieces for four blocks—each 13½ in. square, plus the seam allowance. Use some of the pillow back fabric for the center squares, one of the pinks for the small inner triangles, and plum for the star triangles. The smallest piece of the cream sprig fabric and the second pink are for the corner triangles, and the other cream sprig fabric is for the triangles surrounding the star. Piece the blocks and press the vertical seams in the same direction across the block. Join the blocks edge to edge into two vertical strips, then join the strips together to make a square. Sew the borders to top and bottom first, then to the sides. Press the seams toward the borders.

■ Lay the patchwork on the batting; baste it in place. Quilt along every seam (see page 159), matching the thread color to the fabric. Remove the basting.

■ Complete as for the pillow on page 108, but when topstitching around the edge of the pillow, match the thread color to the fabric.

Lady of the Lake floor pillow

This bold, graphic design works best using strongly contrasting plain or small-scale patterned fabrics. Use furnishing-weight fabrics, as they will take more wear and tear.

Size of pillow: 26 in. square
Size of finished block: 11 in. square

■ From teal fabric, cut two back pieces measuring 27½ x 22 in. and 27½ x 7½ in. respectively.

■ With right sides together, baste the two back pieces together along one long side, taking a ½-in. seam. Machine stitch from each corner for 1½ in. Press the seam open and lay the zipper right side down on the wrong side of the seam. Baste and machine stitch the zipper in place. Remove the basting.

■ Cut two borders in cream and two in teal, each measuring 28 x 3¾ in. These are larger than needed, but it is easier to trim them to size later.

■ Referring to the Lady of the Lake block (see page 22), draft the templates and cut the pieces for four blocks—each 11 in. square, plus the seam allowance. If the fabric

has a pattern or texture direction, it is best to keep this uniform across the cushion.

■ Piece the blocks and press the seams toward the darker fabric on the small triangle squares, then toward the larger triangles. Sew the blocks together edge to edge into two vertical strips, then sew the strips together to make a square. Add the borders—teal to the teal edges first, then the cream edges. Press the seams toward the borders.

■ Lay the patchwork on the batting and baste it in place. Quilt along every seam (see page 159), matching the thread color to the fabric. Remove the basting. Trim the pillow front and back to 27 in. square.

■ Pin the patchwork right side down on the pillow back, with the zipper open. Machine stitch all around, snip off excess fabric on the corners, and turn the cover right side out. Topstitch around the edge of the pillow, again matching the thread color to the fabric.

You will need

- *1 yd teal furnishing-weight fabric*
- *20 in. cream furnishing-weight fabric*
- *25-in. zipper*
- *27½-in. square of 2-oz polyester batting*
- *26-in. square pillow form*
- *Matching thread*

Broken Dishes drawstring bag

The bag is made of canvas-weight checked and striped fabrics. Choosing fabrics with woven, rather than printed, designs ensures that checks and stripes follow the grain of the fabric. Tartans and old-fashioned pillow ticking in blue, brown, or black are perfect.

Size of bag: 13 x 14½ in.
Size of finished block: 6 in. square

■ Referring to the Broken Dishes block (see page 11), make a block 6 in. square, plus the seam allowance.

■ With right sides together, pin the frame strip along the top edge of the block and machine stitch, cutting off the excess at the end of this side. Repeat along the bottom of the block, again cutting off the excess. Finally, sew the checked fabric to the sides. Press the seams away from the block.

■ Cut the back of the bag 14 x 15½ in., then 3 strips 2¾ in. wide and one 5½ in. wide for the bag top from the remaining width. Add them to the patchwork as for the frame. Press seams away from the block.

■ Baste the patchwork backing fabric to the back of the patchwork, and topstitch the seams.

You will need

- 14 in. checked canvas for the back, borders, and block
- 2 x 33-in. strip of small checked fabric for the frame
- 4-in. square of striped fabric and 8-in. square piece of navy fabric for the patchwork
- 14 x 15½ in. piece of fabric for the patchwork backing
- 32-in. length of cord
- Matching thread

■ With right sides together, stitch the front to the back, taking a ½ in. seam, leaving 2½ in. unstitched at the top of each side.

■ Press the tops of the seams open, fold the unstitched edges under and topstitch to neaten.

■ Turn the bag right side out. Fold the top of the bag down into the bag by 2 in., fold the raw edge under by ½ in. and stitch by machine. This will give a channel through which to thread the cord.

Beach duffel bag

Although it is called Nelson's Victory, this patchwork border design resembles beach huts, the blue and cream stripes and checks looking like sun and shadow on wooden boards, with a dark blue sky and gingham sea. The bag is quilted and lined in cotton. Lining it with shower-proof fabric or oilcloth would make it perfect for wet swimming suits.

Size of bag: 17¾ in. tall

■ Referring to the Nelson's Victory border pattern (see page 62), draft and piece a border 6¼ in. deep, finished size. There will be six striped and six mirror-image checked patches in all.

You will need

- 8 x 24 in. each of large-checked and striped fabrics for the patchwork
- 27½ in. small-checked furnishing-weight fabric
- 15 in. navy furnishing-weight fabric or canvas
- 29½ in. lining fabric
- 38¼ x 15 in. piece of 2-oz polyester batting
- Matching thread

■ Cut the remaining fabric for the bag. From checked furnishing fabric, cut a 11 x 38¼-in. piece for the top of the bag, a 3½ x 38¼-in. piece for the bottom of the bag, a base circle with a radius of 6 in., and a 5 x 3-in. strip folded and stitched lengthwise for the strap loop.

■ From across the width of the navy fabric, cut a patchwork border strip measuring 2 x 38¼ in. Also from across the width of the navy fabric, cut two strips for the strap 3 x 32-in., sew together, and press the seam open. Fold lengthwise, turn under the raw edges, and topstitch the whole length.

■ From the lining fabric, cut a piece measuring 17 x 38¼ in. and a circle with a radius of 6 in.

■ Sew the fabrics together in the following order along one long edge, taking a ½ in. seam—lining fabric, wide checked strip, patchworked strip, narrow navy strip, and narrow checked strip. Press the seams away from the patchwork.

■ Pin the batting so that it comes halfway up the top checked strip and quilt along the seams. (Note that you're only stitching through the batting and outer bag fabric—not the lining.)

■ With right sides together, stitch the side seam, making a tube and leaving a gap of 5 in. in the checked fabric just above the lining. Press the seam open.

■ Pin and stitch the lining circle to the lining and the checked circle to the lower edge of the bag, taking a ½ in. seam, with the strap loop folded and poking out to the right side of the bag near the side seam.

■ Fold in the fabric on either side of the gap so that it is level with the side seam to neaten, then turn the bag right side out through the gap.

■ Fold the top 2½ in. of the checked fabric down into the inside of the bag, pin in place and topstitch level with the lining seam to form a channel for the strap.

■ Thread the strap through both the channel and the loop at the bottom of the bag and stitch the two ends together. (You will need to undo the fold stitching a little and restitch it when you have joined the two ends of the strap in order to make the join lie flat.)

Dog Tooth Split sunglasses case

This design is perfect for the seaside! The case is quilted and lined to protect your sunglasses from damage.

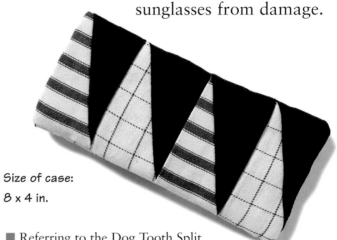

Size of case:
8 x 4 in.

■ Referring to the Dog Tooth Split patchwork border (see page 61), draft and piece two strips of eight triangles. The base of the triangles should be 2 in. and the height 4 in. finished size.

■ Cut the batting in half, then pin one piece to the back of each piece of patchwork. Quilt along the seams on the right side.

■ Cut the lining fabric in half, then stitch one piece to a short end of each of the patchwork strips. With right sides together, sew the two sides of the bag together around the two long and one short sides, leaving a 2-in. gap in the lining on one side. Turn right side out and topstitch the gap closed.

You will need

- 10-in. square of each of navy, striped, and checked furnishing-weight fabrics
- 9-in. square of lining fabric
- 9-in. square of batting
- Matching thread

Log Cabin needle book

This pretty needle book has four felt pages for sewing needles. Foundation blocks are easy to work on a small scale—and the foundation fabric gives a stiffness to the Log Cabin cover.

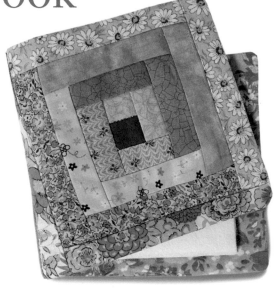

Size of case: 5½ in. square

■ Referring to the Log Cabin block (see pages 54–55), draft and make two 5½-in. square blocks. Trim the foundation fabric to size and stitch the blocks together, side by side (or use a plain square of fabric for the back).

You will need

- Scraps of fabric for the patchwork
- Two 6-in. squares of cotton foundation fabric
- 12- x 6-in. piece of lining fabric
- Two 4¾- x 9½-in. pieces of felt
- Matching thread

■ With right sides together, stitch the patchwork to the lining, leaving a 2-in. gap in the lower edge. Turn right side out through the gap and hand stitch the gap closed.

■ With the inside of the book facing upward, center and pin the two sheets of felt in place, and machine stitch down the center, along the "spine" of the book.

Big Dipper pincushion

Although you could use any patchwork block, Big Dipper is easy to draft and piece on a small scale and can even be worked with every triangle in a different scrap of fabric.

Size of pincushion: 6 in. square

You will need

- Eight pieces of bright cottons, each 4 in. square
- Leftover scraps of batting
- Matching thread

■ Referring to the Big Dipper block (see page 13), draft and make two blocks, 6 in. square.

■ With right sides together, stitch the two sides of the cushion together, leaving a 2-in. gap in one side. Turn right side out through the gap, fill with batting, and hand stitch the gap closed.

Pineapple sewing box lid

Pineapple patchwork has alternating strips of pale and darker-toned fabric to make the design work. Using just two strongly contrasting fabrics gives a dramatic effect; using fabrics close in tone gives the appearance of basket weave.

Size of lid: 9¾ in. across

■ Referring to the Pineapple block (see page 56), draft and make a block 10½ in. wide. The center square on this one measures 1½ in. when stitched, and there are seven dark and light strips. You won't need to fill out the dark corners as the block will be trimmed to a 10½-in. diameter circle.

■ Stitch the ends of the border strip together, leaving a 1-in. gap for inserting the elastic. Fold in half lengthwise and stitch it to the outside edge of the trimmed patchwork.

You will need

● Scraps of fabric 1⅛ in. wide for the patchwork
● 31- x 3-in. piece of cream sprig fabric for the border and a 10½-in. diameter circle of cream sprig fabric for the lining
● 12-in. square of foundation fabric
● 27½-in. length of narrow elastic
● Matching thread

■ With right sides together, lay the lining circle on top of the patchwork, the border strip sandwiched between, and stitch, leaving a 2-in. gap. Turn right side out and hand stitch the gap. Thread the elastic through the gap in the border, and hand stitch the gap closed.

Four-patch sampler quilt

Sampler quilts can be made of any number of different quilt blocks—appliqué, or patchwork, or a combination. Keeping to the same grid blocks (four-, five-, seven-, or nine-patch) gives uniformity. This quilt uses all the larger four-patch blocks, with Odd Fellow's Chain in the center.

Size of quilt: 61 in. square
Size of each finished block: 12 in. square;
central block 24 in. square
Width of border and sashing: 2½ in.;
frame around central block 2 in.

■ Referring to the four-patch block section (see pages 10–27), draft and piece 12 surround blocks to the sizes described. This sampler quilt contains Ann and Andy, Triangle Squares, Double X, Indian Star, Crystal Star, Diamond Star, Chevron, Flying Geese, Batchelor's Puzzle, Mosaic, Old Maid's Puzzle, Flower Basket, with Odd Fellow's Chain as the center block.

■ Cut the pale yellow fabric for the center frame into strips 1¾ in. wide and join to make a continuous strip.

With right sides together, join the strip to the sides of the center block, trimming off the excess, and then to the top and bottom edges. Press the seams away from the block.

■ Take 43 in. of the yellow striped fabric for the sashing and borders, cut it into 14 3-in. strips across the width of the fabric, and sew into one continuous length.

■ Lay the blocks out in sequence. Sew the top middle pair and the bottom middle pair together horizontally edge to edge, with a length of sashing (cut from the long strip) in between each block, and press the seams toward the sashing. Stitch a sashing strip to the upper and lower edges of the center block and join the upper and lower pairs to this. Press the seams toward the sashing.

■ Sash the left- and right-hand edges of the central piece. Join the four left- and right-hand side blocks into a vertical strip, with a length of sashing in between each block. Join these strips to the left and right of the center block. Press the seams toward the sashing.

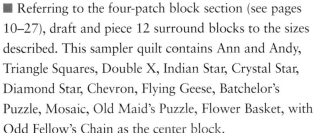

You will need

● *3 yd in total of plain colorful fabrics for the blocks*
● *8 in. pale yellow cotton fabric for the center frame*
● *59 in. yellow striped cotton fabric for the sashing, borders, and binding*
● *67-in. square of cotton fabric, or equivalent seamed, for the backing*
● *67-in. square of 2-oz polyester batting*
● *Matching thread*

■ Sew lengths of the sashing to the side edges of the quilt and then to the top and bottom edges. Press the seams away from the blocks.

■ Lay the backing wrong side up and cover with the batting. Lay the quilt top right side up on the batting and backing, and baste through all three layers, in a vertical, horizontal, and diagonal grid.

■ Quilt "in the ditch" or just next to it, over the seam for extra strength (see page 159), in thread that matches the fabrics.

■ Trim off any excess batting and backing fabric.

■ Cut the remaining yellow striped fabric into six strips 2½ in. wide and join into one length for the binding. Fold under and press ½ in. along one long edge. Bind the quilt from the back (see page 172), adding a little of the batting remnants as you proceed.

Nine-patch framed quilt in printed lawns

This 25-block quilt has a repeat design of Nine Patch blocks, with alternating dark and light frames. The Nine Patch blocks and many of the inner frames are random. In all, about 50 fabrics are used; it is advisable to buy full-width fabric, not "fat quarters" for this.

Size of quilt: 95 in. square
Size of each finished block: 18½ in. square

■ Cut 225 2¾-in. squares for the blocks. Piece 25 Nine Patch blocks (see page 29) in a variety of color combinations.

■ Now cut the rest of the fabric into 2½-in. strips across the fabric width, and sew together to make continuous lengths of each fabric. Lawn is very light and these fabrics are highly patterned, so seams in the strips will not detract from the design and will make the most economical use of the fabric. Put aside the four darks and pales for the borders and binding fabric for later.

■ Using the palest fabrics first, frame each block; first add the sides, cutting the strip to length, and then the top and bottom. Press the seams outward.

■ The second frame is made up of two different fabrics, which are best attached in Log Cabin style (see pages 54–55)—piecing a first and second strip clockwise around the block in one fabric and the third and fourth in a different fabric.

■ Finally, use the pales and darks for the outer frames. Lay the blocks out in five rows of five and decide whether a pale or a dark frame would work best for each one. Alternate light and dark frames across the quilt. The outer frames are not random, so keep to your chosen sequence throughout.

■ Piece the blocks into five vertical strips and press the seams in alternate directions. Sew these strips together and press the seams in the same direction across the quilt.

■ To quilt, center the batting on the backing fabric and then center the quilt top on top. Baste through all three layers, vertically, horizontally, and diagonally (see page 157). Starting in the center of the central block, machine or hand quilt over every seam, quilting the nine-patch seams first and then the frames. Leave quilting the seams that join the blocks until the end.

■ Remove the basting thread carefully—it may be caught by machine-quilting stitches.

■ Trim off the excess batting and backing.

You will need

- 1 yd each of two dark and two pale fabrics for the outer block frames
- 5½ yd in total of a variety of harmonizing fabrics for blocks
- 30 in. dark fabric for the binding
- 102-in. square of white or colored cotton, or the equivalent seamed, for the backing
- 102-in. square of 2-oz polyester batting
- Matching thread

Cut the binding fabric into strips 2½ in. wide across the width of the fabric. Sew them together to make a continuous strip and press the seams. Fold over one long edge by about ½ in. and press. Bind the quilt from the back (see page 172), adding a little of the batting remnants as you proceed.

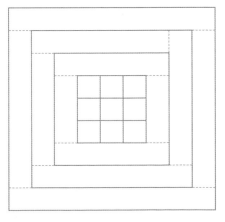

Fly block crib quilt

This is a soft and warm crib quilt in blues and greens. The plain and simple blue and green fabrics contrast with the busy design of the blue rose design fabric. The quilt is four blocks across and four down, with top and lower edge borders made up of random triangle squares.

Size of quilt: 30 x 41½ in.
Size of each finished block: 7 in.

■ Referring to the Fly block (see page 12), draft and make six blue floral/mid-blue blocks, five floral/pale blue blocks, and five floral/green blocks. Piece 16 random 3½-in. triangle squares from the leftovers and join them into two strips.

You will need

- 30 in. blue floral fabric
- 20 in. each of mid blue and pale blue cotton fabric
- 10 in. green cotton
- Two contrasting strips 3 in. wide, cut across the width of the fabric, for the top and bottom sashing
- 34- x 45½-in. piece of cotton fabric for backing
- 34- x 45½-in. piece of 2-oz polyester batting
- 10 in. binding fabric
- Matching thread

■ Lay the blocks out in sequence, with four blocks across and four down, and assemble. Sash the top and bottom edges with the contrasting strips and join the strips of triangle squares to the top and bottom edges. Press the seams toward the sashing.

■ Center the batting on the backing fabric and then center the quilt top on top. Baste through all three layers, vertically, horizontally, and diagonally (see page 157).

■ Quilt along every seam (see page 159). Remove the basting thread carefully—it may be caught by machine-quilting stitches.

■ Cut the fabric for the binding across the width of the fabric into four strips 2½ in. wide, fold one long edge over by about ½ in., and press the entire length.

■ Bind the quilt from the back (see page 172), adding a little of the batting remnants as you proceed.

Tumbling Blocks baby quilt

This is a soft baby quilt made from printed lawns. It is a good design for using a multitude of scraps, provided they are in pale, mid, and dark tones. It can be worked over papers, seamed by hand or by machine. The backing fabric is folded over to the front as the binding.

Size of quilt: 19½ x 25 in.
Length of each finished diamond: 3½ in.

■ Referring to the Tumbling Blocks block (see page 43), draft and piece 32 blocks; the diamond should be 3½ in. long when stitched.

■ Cut 12 extra diamonds in a pale color to even out the top and bottom edges and, using a finished block as template, six half hexagons for the side edges.

■ Lay all the blocks out in sequence. For rows 1, 3, 5, and 7, you will need five whole blocks; for rows 2, 4, 6, you will need four whole blocks. Start in a corner and sew two blocks together side by side, then add a third one below them. Next, piece a block to the right of the lower one and a fourth below this pair, always trying to

have just two edges to stitch each time. Finally, level the edges by adding the extra diamonds and half hexagons. Press all the seams in the same direction across the quilt.

■ Center the quilt top on the batting and backing. Baste through all three layers vertically, horizontally, and diagonally (see page 157).

■ Quilt "in the ditch" (see page 159) of every seam.

■ Starting with top and bottom edges, fold the batting and backing over to the front of the quilt. Fold under the edge of the backing fabric, and topstitch by machine or slipstitch by hand. Repeat on the side edges. The excess batting will make the binding slightly puffy.

You will need

- 6 in. each of four pale, four mid, and four dark tones of cotton fabric for the whole blocks
- 12 in. cotton fabric for the part blocks around the edge
- 25- x 30½-in. piece of cotton fabric for the backing
- 25- x 30½-in. piece of 2-oz polyester batting
- Matching thread

Double Irish Chain quilt

This is a five-patch block with two blocks to draft and piece—one mainly white, the other mainly colored. The chain design appears when the alternating blocks are pieced edge to edge. An opaque white fabric avoids show-through.

Size of quilt: 75 x 75 in.
Size of each finished block: 15 in. square

■ A quilt needs an odd number of blocks across and down for the design to be symmetrical, so measure the bed and bed drop and divide into 3, 5, 7, or 9 to work out the size of block that you need. The blocks are best made 9–15 in. square.

■ Referring to the Double Irish Chain block on page 26, draft and make 13 blocks with a blue and green checkered pattern and 12 white blocks with blue corners. Because the checkered patches are alternated with white, you may have to trim excess dark fabric from the seams to avoid show-through.

■ Lay the blocks out in five rows of five. The first, middle and last strip should have checkered blocks top and bottom, while the second and fourth strips should

have white blocks top and bottom. Piece the blocks edge to edge in five vertical strips. Press the seams in alternate directions from strip to strip.

■ Assemble the strips and press all the vertical seams in one direction across the quilt.

■ Lay the backing wrong side up on your work surface, with the batting on top (see pages 156–159). Lay the quilt top right side up on the batting and backing. Baste well, in a vertical, horizontal, and diagonal grid. Quilt "in the ditch" or over the seams, matching the thread to the patch color if you are quilting by machine. If you are quilting by hand, use white thread throughout.

■ Trim off the excess batting and backing.

■ Cut eight binding strips 2 in. wide across the width of the fabric and sew together end to end in pairs. Fold under and press ½ in. along one long edge.

■ Bind the quilt from the back (see page 172), adding a little of the batting remnants as you proceed.

You will need

- 79 in. blue cotton fabric for the blocks and binding
- 36 in. green cotton fabric
- 90 in. white cotton fabric
- 83-in. square (or equivalent seamed) of cotton fabric for the backing
- 83-in. square 2-oz polyester batting
- Matching thread (or white thread, if hand quilting)

Grandmother's Fan coverlet

This heavily padded coverlet, with vintage pink and cream toile de Jouy sashing, is four blocks across and four down, with a wide binding. The backing fabric on the blocks is a rich cream and the quarter circles are dark pink to match the toile de Jouy. The soft floral fabrics on the fan are in keeping with the vintage fabric.

Size of quilt: 62 in. square
Size of finished block: 11 in. square

■ Referring to the Grandmother's Fan block (see page 52), draft and make sixteen blocks. Trim to 11½ in. square.

■ The toile de Jouy has a distinct pattern direction that needs to be kept uniform across the quilt. Cut three binding strips 7 in. wide from the length of the toile de Jouy and sew them all together to make one continuous strip. Fold one long edge over by about ½ in. and press the entire length.

■ Cutting across the width of the remaining fabric, cut twelve sashing strips measuring 4¾ x 12 in. Finally, cut three sashing strips from the length of the remaining fabric, 4¾ in. wide.

■ Piece sets of four blocks into vertical strips, with short lengths of sashing in between. Sew the strips together with sashing. Press the seams toward the sashing.

■ Center the batting on the backing fabric and then center the quilt top on top. Baste through all three layers, vertically, horizontally, and diagonally (see page 157).

■ Quilt around the quarter circle curves and then about ¼ in. away from the patchwork and sashing on the cream

backing fabric. Finally, quilt ¼ in. away from the seams on the sashing fabric.

■ Remove the basting carefully—it may be caught by machine-quilting stitches.

■ Trim off the excess batting and backing. Bind the quilt from the back (see page 172), adding strips of batting remnants as you proceed.

Broken Circles quilt

This nine-block quilt has rings of varied widths, which don't match up. It is made from silk, which is easy to work with as it takes a crease well and is light to work. As long as the silk is even-weave, you can vary the direction of the grain; then the silk will seem to change color as the light catches the different direction of weave.

Size of quilt: 56 in. square
Size of each finished block: 18 in. square

■ Referring to the Broken Circles block (see page 51), draft four quarter-block templates, each with rings of different radii as follows:
Quarter block A: 3½ and 5½ in.
Quarter block B: 4½ and 7½ in.
Quarter block C: 5 and 8¼ in.
Quarter block D: 2½ and 6 in.

■ When you make the cardboard templates, add a ¼-in. seam allowance.

■ Cut the fabric, alternating colors for the outer and inner rings, and label each fabric piece A, B, C, or D. Although the color combinations are random, 12 quarter blocks have red on the outside, 12 cream, eight blue, and four green.

■ Piece the patches and blocks as shown on page 51.

You will need

● 1½ yrds each of red and cream silk dupioni for the blocks
● 1 yd each of blue, green, and black silk dupioni for the blocks
● ½ yd black silk dupioni for the binding
● 60-in. square of 4-oz (135-g) polyester batting
● 64-in. square of cotton fabric, or the equivalent seamed, for the backing
● Matching thread

■ Lay the blocks out in random sequence, piece into vertical strips and press the seams in alternate directions. Sew the strips together and press.

■ Center the batting on the backing fabric, then center the quilt top on top. Baste through all three layers vertically, horizontally, and diagonally (see page 157).

■ Machine or hand quilt "in the ditch" (see page 159), using harmonizing threads. First quilt the quarter circles (both the curve and the straight lines) in the center block, and then quilt the rings (both the curve and the straight lines). Working one block at a time, quilt the quarter circles and rings on the remaining blocks. Quilt the blocks at the top and bottom of the quilt first, then those either side of the center one. Finally, quilt the remaining straight lines, starting from the center seams and working outward. Remove the basting carefully; it may be caught by machine-quilting stitches.

■ Trim off the excess batting and backing, leaving it extending about ½ in. beyond the quilt top.

■ Cut binding strips 3½ in. wide across the width of the black silk and sew them together in a continuous strip. Press the seams flat, fold one long edge over by about ½ in., and press the entire length. Bind from the front (see page 173), adding some of the batting remnants as you proceed.

Sewing order

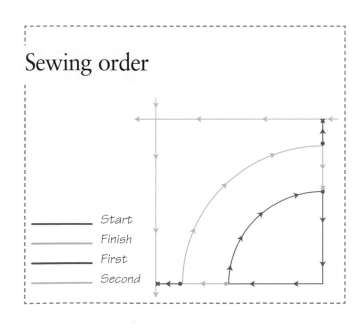

Start
Finish
First
Second

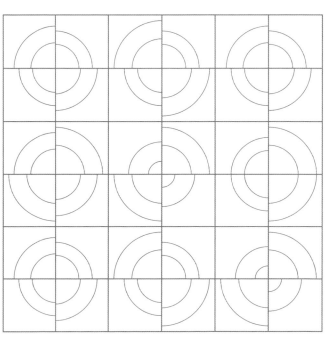

Christmas cards

Use cottons, silks, satins, or even velvets for the backgrounds and appliqué. Try out metallic or rainbow threads and add beads and buttons. The Holly leaf and Dove designs (pages 66–69) would also work as Christmas-card motifs.

You will need

- Scraps of fabric for the appliqué
- 8¼- x 6-in. piece of light background fabric such as cotton, silk, or satin
- 8¼- x 6-in. three-fold card with 6½- x 4-in. apertures
- Double-sided tape
- Matching thread

■ Referring to the Christmas motifs (see page 82), draft and appliqué the tree and snowman onto the background fabrics. The tree is stitched onto a satin block 3½ x 5 in. with a checked frame and has beads hand stitched on for festive sparkle, while the snowman is on a variegated wintry blues cotton rainbow fabric and is padded and outline quilted.

■ Trim the fabric to about ½ in. larger all around than the aperture in the card. Open up the card blank, apply double-sided tape around the edges of the aperture, place the appliqué piece right side down on top and press down to fix the fabric in place. Apply more tape around the edges of the appliqué piece, then fold over the left-hand panel of the card and press down firmly.

Fancy Fish album cover

This removable quilted cover is designed to fit an album measuring roughly 13 x 10 in., but you could easily adapt it to suit other dimensions. You could also substitute other motifs to suit the occasion—entwined monograms for a wedding album, perhaps.

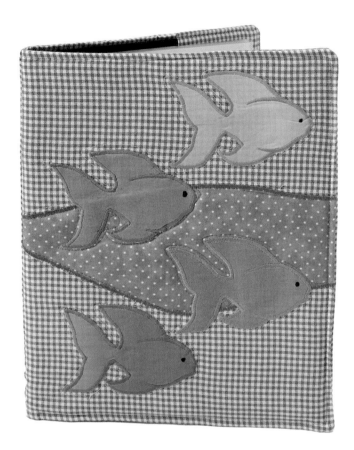

Size of album cover: 13 x 10 in.
½ in. seam allowance throughout

You will need

- 24 in. blue gingham
- 11½- x 6-in. piece of blue dotted cotton fabric for the wave
- Scraps of brightly colored fabric for the fish
- 22- x 14-in. piece of 2-oz polyester batting
- Matching thread

■ From blue gingham fabric, cut one 22 x 14-in. piece for the lining, two 11½ x 14-in. pieces for the front and back, and two 8½ x 14-in. pieces for the inside flaps. Fold and press the inside flaps to 4¼ x 14 in.

■ Lay the blue spot fabric on the front cover fabric about midway down. Using tailor's chalk, draw two wavy lines across the blue spot fabric, then cut out. Pin to the cover fabric and satin stitch it in place, setting the stitch width to 3.

■ Using the Fancy Fish template on page 85, cut out four fish motifs. (I used a variegated, rainbow fabric.) Appliqué the fish to the front of the cover. I varied the outline thread colour. Press from the back.

■ Stitch together the back and front covers along one long edge, taking a ½-in. seam, and press.

■ Lay the cover right side up on top of the batting and baste the two layers together (see page 157).

■ Quilt around the fish, about ¼ in. away from the motifs and along the wave fabric, making sure you do not stitch over the fish. Vary the thread color to match the gingham and blue spot fabric.

■ Lay the quilted piece on your work surface, right side up. Place the flaps at each side, with the folded edge towards the center, and lay the lining on top. Pin through all layers. Machine stitch, taking a ½-in. seam, leaving a 4-in. gap at the bottom. Trim the edges and corners, turn right side out, hand stitch the gap closed, and then machine top stitch very close to the edge all the way around.

Child's counting quilt

This quilt or crawl mat has lots of colors, patterns, and shapes to discover and count. Use snippets from other projects or clothing to make it more personal to the child.

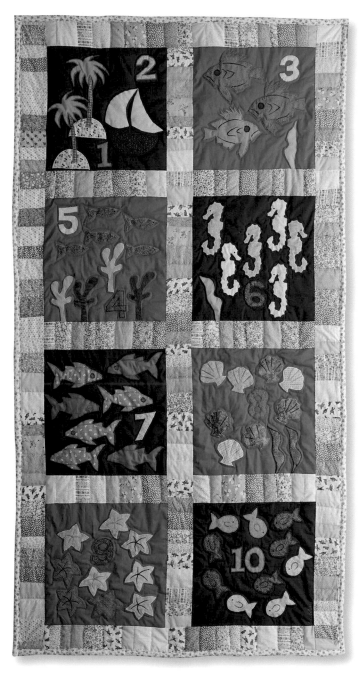

Size of quilt: 78 x 41¾ in.
Size of each finished block: 15 in. square
Border and sashing: 3½ in. wide
¼ in. seam allowance throughout

■ Cut four 17½-in. squares of each of the two block backing fabrics. These will be trimmed to size after stitching.

■ Using the templates on pages 84–85 and 96, transfer the required number of motifs onto brightly colored scraps of fabric and cut out. Machine or hand appliqué the motifs onto the turquoise and blue backing fabrics, alternating the color of the backing fabrics and making sure the numbers are in the right order. Press from the back and trim the backing fabrics to size and shape, to 15½ in. square.

■ To make the sashing and borders, cut widthwise into strips 2–2¾ in. wide. Machine stitch the strips together in a random order into blocks of about ten strips. Press all the seams one way. With the strips running horizontally, cut these newly formed blocks of joined strips vertically into strips 4⅛ in. wide. Piece them together to form a

You will need

- 1 yd each of blue and turquoise cotton fabrics to back the blocks
- Bright scraps for the motifs
- 60 in. in total of at least 10 different fabrics for the borders and sashing
- 2½ yd cotton fabric for the backing
- 2½ yd of 2-oz polyester batting
- 24 in. cotton fabric for the binding
- Matching thread

long strip about 12½ yd long, making sure that all the seams are in the same direction.

■ Lay the appliquéd blocks out in sequence. Piece the left-hand blocks into a vertical strip, with a length of sashing (cut from the long strip) in between each block. Repeat with the right-hand blocks. Press the seams toward the sashing. Piece the two vertical block strips with a length of sashing, and press the seams toward the sashing. Sew lengths of the sashing border to the top and lower edges of the quilt, and then to the side edges. Press the seams away from the blocks.

■ Lay the backing wrong side up and cover with the batting. Lay the quilt top right side up on the batting and backing, and baste well, in a vertical, horizontal, and diagonal grid.

■ Outline quilt the motifs (see page 159), stitching about ¼ in. away in thread that matches the backings, then quilt "in the ditch" or just next to it, over the seams for extra strength.

■ Trim off any excess batting and backing fabric.

■ Cut the binding fabric into 3-in. strips across the width of the fabric and sew together into a continuous strip. Press the seams. Fold over one long edge by about ½ in. and press. Bind the quilt from the back, padding with strips of batting as you proceed.

Cat blanket

Perfect for cat lovers, this simple little blanket will brighten up any armchair. Make it from washable furnishing fabric that blends with your color scheme.

Size of blanket: 32 In. square
Satin stitch width: 3

■ Referring to the Sleeping Cat block (see page 77), draft and cut out the cat motif. As the motif is large, make sure that the grain of the cat fabric matches that of the background fabric. Appliqué the cat to the background, and work the face details last.

■ Turn under a double fold of ½ in. all the way around, baste and press flat. On the right side, satin stitch all the way around, about ¼ in. from the edge.

You will need

- 12-in. square of plain-colored furnishing-weight fabric for the cat
- 34-in. square of patterned furnishing-weight fabric for the background
- Matching thread

Farmyard quilt

With its appliquéd farmyard animals and Barn Fence border, this makes a really colorful and cheery quilt for a child's room.

Size of quilt: 25 x 33 in.

Width of border: 4 in.

¼ in. seam allowance throughout

■ Lay background strips one above another, overlapping, so overall length is 25½ in. Draw a curve on the top edge of lowest strip (make sure the curve doesn't extend beyond the overlap), cut the curve and pin to the fabric above. Repeat all the way up. Satin stitch the curvy strips. Press and trim the excess fabric away on the back.

■ Using the templates on pages 78–81, transfer the required number of motifs onto brightly colored scraps of fabric and cut out. Pin and appliqué them onto the background fabrics. Press from the back and trim to 16⅜ x 24¼ in.

■ Referring to the Barn Fence block (see page 36), cut strips 1½ x 4¼ in. and piece into 24 blocks of four different colored strips. Press all the seams in one direction and then piece edge to edge, rotating in alternate directions, to make four borders six blocks long. Press all the seams in the same direction. Attach the side borders to the quilt top first, then add the top and bottom borders. Press the seams outward.

■ Lay the backing wrong side up and cover with the batting. Lay the quilt top right side up on the batting and backing, and baste well, in a vertical, horizontal, and diagonal grid.

■ Outline quilt the motifs (see page 159), stitching about ¼ in. away in thread that matches the backgrounds, then quilt over every short seam of the border. Trim off any excess batting and backing fabric.

■ Cut the binding fabric into three 2½-in. strips across the width of the fabric and sew into a continuous strip. Press the seams. Fold over one long edge by about ½ in. and press. Bind from the back (see page 172), padding with strips of batting as you proceed.

You will need

● Five 18- x 8½-in. pieces of cotton fabric—two in green spots for the field backgrounds, two in green checks, and one in blue for the sky
● Bright fabric scraps for the motifs
● 8 in. fabric in four colors for the borders
● 27 x 35½ in. cotton for the backing
● 27- x 35½-in. piece of 2-oz polyester batting
● 8 in. green checked fabric for the binding
● Matching thread

Rooster hanging

This hanging is made from cottons with a furnishing-weight or linen backing panel, and is finished with a triangle squares patchwork border. Easy to wash, it is suitable for a kitchen.

Size of hanging: 18 x 20 in.

¼ in. seam allowance throughout

■ Draft, cut, and make the Rooster block, following the instructions on pages 74–75. Trim the backing fabric to 13 x 15 in.

■ From scraps in random combinations, draft and make 22 triangle squares for the 2½ in. Sawtooth border (see page 58) and four 2½ in. corner squares with split triangles (see page 24).

■ Piece five triangle squares together in a strip and join to the top edge of the block. Repeat on the lower edge. Press the seams away from the block.

■ Piece the remaining triangle squares into two strips of six, and add a split triangle square to each end of each strip. Sew these strips to the sides of the block. Press the seams away from the block.

You will need

- Four fabrics 8 in. square for the body, tails and ruff pieces, and three pieces 4 in. square for the leg, feet and beak, and comb
- 14- x 16-in. piece of furnishing-weight fabric or linen for the backing
- 20- x 21½-in. piece of lining fabric or calico for the back of the hanging
- 26 assorted scraps at least 3½ in. square for the patchwork border
- 20- x 21½-in. piece of 2-oz polyester batting
- Four 2- x 21-in. strips for the binding
- Matching thread

■ Place the backing fabric right side down on your work surface, with the batting on top, and the appliqué block right side up on top of the batting. Baste the layers together; the batting and backing should be about 1 in. larger than the front.

■ Outline quilt the rooster (see page 159), stitching about ¼ in. from the motif. Quilt the patchwork border along the diagonal and straight seams, either "in the ditch" or on the seams.

■ Trim off the excess backing and batting.

■ Bind the edges from the back (see page 172).

Lavender bag with hearts

This pretty little cotton bag with hand-appliquéd hearts for fresh lavender or potpourri, can be washed and refilled when the scent evaporates.

Size of bag: 8 x 4 in.

½ in. seam allowance throughout

■ Referring to the Heart motifs (see page 68), draft and cut out two hearts—the larger one 2¾ in. across and the smaller one 2 in. across—and add a turning allowance. Hand appliqué first the larger one and then, on top and centered, the smaller one onto one piece of background fabric (see pages 166–167), using thread that matches the darkest color of the motifs.

■ Turn under and press one long edge of the top bands by ½ in. and machine stitch the right side of the raw edge to the wrong side of the bag tops. Fold the fabric over to the front and topstitch.

■ With right sides together, stitch together the sides and bottom of the bag. Turn right side out.

■ To make the tie, cut a 10 x 1-in. strip of the contrasting band fabric. Fold it in half, stitch along the length, and turn right side out. Turn under and hand stitch the short ends.

You will need

- Two 4-in. squares of cotton fabric in pale and darker colors for the hearts
- Two 7- x 4¾-in. pieces of background fabric
- Two 3- x 4¾-in. strips of darker-toned patterned fabric for the tops of the bags
- 10- x 1-in. strip of darker-toned patterned fabric for the tie
- Matching thread

Make-up bag with butterflies

This soft, padded zipper bag in linen and cotton has a
hand-appliquéd butterfly panel on the front; you could stitch
a second panel for the back with dragonflies or bees. Line it
with shower-proof fabric to make it durable.

Size of bag: 9 x 13½ in.

Size of finished block: 5½ x 10 in.

½ in. seam allowance throughout

■ Referring to the Butterfly motifs on page
65, draft, cut, and appliqué the motifs onto
the background fabric. Press from the back
and trim to 6¼ x 10½ in.

■ Cut a 9¾ x 14-in. bag back, two strips
measuring 2¾ x 9¾ in. from across the width
of fabric for the side borders, and two strips
measuring 2¾ x 10½ in. from the length of
the fabric for the top and bottom borders. Stitch
the top and bottom borders and press the seams
outward. Then add the side borders and press the
seams outward.

■ Baste the front of the bag to the batting. Outline quilt
the motifs and quilt along the border seams, by hand or
machine (see pages 158–159).

■ Baste the front and back pieces together along the top,
using the seam allowance. Taking a ½-in. seam, machine
stitch from each corner for ½ in. Press the seam open and
lay the zipper right side down on the wrong side of the
seam. Baste and then machine stitch the zipper in place.
Remove the basting.

■ With right sides together, stitch the front of the bag to
the back. Pinch the seams together at the bottom and
stitch across to make a base.

■ Stitch three sides of the lining and hand sew it to the
inside of the bag, just covering the zipper stitching.

You will need

- Scraps of small-patterned cotton fabric for the
  appliqué
- 7 x 11½-in. piece of blue linen fabric for the
  background
- 10½ in. striped cotton fabric for the back
  and borders
- Two 9¾- x 14-in. pieces of lining fabric
- 9¾- x 14-in. piece of 2-oz polyester batting
- 12-in. zipper
- Matching thread

Dragonfly pouch

This hand-appliquéd pouch makes a beautiful nightgown or stockings case. The pouch itself is made from linen, which has a soft feel and looks good even when crumpled and creased. Use lightweight cottons or lawns for the appliqué motifs.

Size of bag: 11½ in. square
Size of finished block: 6 in. square
½ in. seam allowance throughout

■ Cut a 8-in. square of blue linen and, referring to the Dragonfly motif (see page 63), draft, cut, and hand appliqué the motifs onto it. Press from the back and then trim to 6¾ in. square.

■ Stitch the frame strip to the side edges, cutting off the excess as you proceed. Press the seams outward. Stitch the frame strip to the top and bottom edges and press the seams outward.

■ Cut the border fabric into 2½-in. strips, sew on as for the frame strips, and press seams toward border.

■ Cut a 12¼ x 18½-in. piece of blue linen for the back of the pouch. With wrong sides together, stitch the block to the pouch back along the top edge and add a strip of border fabric to the bottom edge of the block. Press the seams away from the backing fabric.

■ Baste the top of the pouch to the batting. Outline quilt, stitching ¼ in. away from the motif, and quilt either "in the ditch" or on the seams (see page 159).

■ With right sides together, stitch the front of the bag to the lining fabric, leaving a 2-in. gap in one edge. Turn the bag right side out, fold the lower part up to make an envelope 7½ in. deep, and topstitch the sides.

You will need

● *Scraps of small-patterned cottons for the appliqué*
● *12¼in. blue linen fabric for the appliqué background and back of the pouch*
● *2-in. strip of blue-and-white cotton fabric for the frame*
● *5-in. strip of blue and pink stripe fabric for the border*
● *12¼- x 32-in. piece of lining fabric*
● *12¼- x 32-in. piece of 2-oz polyester batting*
● *Matching thread*

Tulip place mat

The wide borders on these place mats are made from the backing fabric folded over to the front. It has a strong medium-scale pattern, similar to the appliqué design itself. Cotton batting inside protects the table from the heat of the plates; it can withstand a high temperature wash and iron.

Size of place mat: 10 x 15¾ in.

Size of block: 7 x 9 in.

½ in. seam allowance throughout

You will need

- Scraps of cotton print fabrics in red, green, and cream for the appliqué
- 8½- x 11-in. piece of appliqué background fabric
- Two 8- x 2-in. strips of border fabric
- 10- x 15¾-in. piece of cotton batting
- 14- x 22-in. piece of backing fabric
- Matching thread

■ Referring to the Tulip Bunch motifs (see pages 64–65), draft, cut, and machine appliqué the motifs onto the background fabric. Trim to 8 x 9¾ in.

■ With right sides together, stitch the border strips to the side edges. Press the seams outward.

■ Center the block on the batting and backing fabric and baste it in place. Outline quilt the motifs and quilt along the border seams (see page 159).

■ Fold over the top and bottom edges of the backing fabric by ½ in. and press, then fold over to the front and topstitch to the block. Repeat with the side edges and hand stitch the corners to secure.

Dove and leaf tablecloth

This square white linen tablecloth has doves along the edges and leaves and a berry on the corners. The crisp ginghams and simple floral prints lend themselves to the traditional stylized motifs, and the colors are reminiscent of old blue-and-white country crockery.

Size of tablecloth: 39 in. square
Satin stitch width: 3

You will need

- Scraps of navy and white gingham, striped, or spotted cotton fabric for the appliqué
- 39-in. square of white linen
- Four 1½- x 41-in. strips of white-and-navy floral cotton fabric for the binding
- Matching thread

■ Referring to the Hearts, Dove, and Tulip motifs (see pages 68–69), draft the templates and cut out the fabric; the birds pictured are 8 in. long, the leaves 4 in. long and the berries have a radius of 1½ in.

■ Fold and crease the linen in four, then open it out and fold the cloth in four again from corner to corner. Use the crease lines to place the motifs symmetrically: one dove midway along each side with branch and leaf tips about 4 in. from the edge and a leaf and berry bunch in each corner. Stitch the motifs in place, using satin stitch width 3 and matching the thread to the darkest color in the motif fabric. Lay the top thread along the line of stitching and stitch over it for about 1 in. to conceal and secure it, then trim. At the end, draw the threads to the back, thread through a needle and pass through the stitched channel and trim.

■ Fold under and press one long edge on each binding strip. Bind from the back (see page 172).

Bread basket napkin with tulip motif

Ties have been added to this linen napkin so that it can be used to line a basket and cover bread or cookies. Use thread that matches the darkest color in the fabrics to make the motifs stand out, and place a tulip in each corner where it will be most visible.

Size of napkin: 19½ in. square
Satin stitch width: 3

■ Referring to the Hearts, Dove, and Tulip motifs (see pages 66–67), draft the templates and cut out the fabric for four tulips; the tulips pictured are 4¼ in. tall. Fold and crease the linen in quarters diagonally and pin each of the four tulips on the fold lines, their points about 2 in. from the edges of the linen.

■ Satin stitch along the fold lines from one tulip base to another, then appliqué the tulips. Draw the threads to the front of the work, trim and conceal under the appliqué. The petals will be the last pieces to stitch; draw these threads to the back, tie, and trim or thread through the satin-stitch channel.

■ Fold under one long edge of each binding strip. Pin and stitch the right side of the shortest binding strip to the back of the napkin, aligning the raw edges and stitch.

You will need

- Scraps of cotton fabric for the appliqué
- 19½-in. square of white linen
- One 20- x 1-in. strip, two 27- x 1-in. strips, and one 34- x 1-in. strip of blue-and-white cotton for the binding and ties
- Matching thread

Fold the folded edge of the binding over to the front and topstitch.

■ Working counterclockwise, take a medium-length strip and bind the next edge in the same way, leaving the excess length at the end for the tie. Bring the binding to the front and topstitch all the way along, including the tie end (fold in the end of the strip and stitch across to neaten). Repeat on the next counterclockwise edge. The final binding strip will extend about 7 in. at both the beginning and end for ties.

Monogrammed pillow

This pillow makes an especially personal gift. The monogram is in small-patterned delicate printed lawn, outlined in thread that matches one of the darker colors in the fabric and contrasts well with the larger scale patterns of the frame and border fabrics.

Size of pillow: 17 in. square
Size of finished block: 7 in. square
½ in. seam allowance throughout

■ Referring to the Appliqué Alphabet (see pages 89–93), draft, cut, and appliqué the motif to the background fabric. Press from the back and trim to 8 in. square.

■ With right sides together, piece the frame strip to the side edges of the block, cutting off the excess as you proceed. Press the seams away from the block, and then add the frame strips to the top and bottom edges.

■ Cut four border strips measuring 4 x 17¾ in. Sew borders to the side edges of the block, and trim off the excess. Then attach borders to the top and bottom edges and press the seams away from the block.

■ Baste the pillow top to the batting. Outline quilt the motif (see page 159), stitching about ¼ in. away, and then quilt over the seams.

You will need

- 6-in. square of cotton print for the appliqué motif
- 9-in. square of cream background fabric
- 3- x 40-in. strip of cotton fabric for the frame
- 18 in. furnishing-weight fabric for the back and borders
- 17-in. square of 2-oz polyester batting
- 16-in. zipper
- 17-in. square pillow form
- Matching thread

■ Cut two 17¾ x 9½-in. pieces of backing fabric. With right sides together, baste the two back pieces together along one long side using the seam allowance. Taking a ½-in. seam, machine stitch from each corner for 1 in.. Press the seam open and lay the zipper right side down on the wrong side of the seam. Baste and then machine stitch the zipper in place. Remove the basting.

■ Open the zipper. With right sides together, stitch together the pillow front and back. Snip off any excess around the edges and corners, turn right side out, and topstitch around the edge of the pillow.

Square pillow with leaf and berry panels

This pillow is made from furnishing fabrics, with the back and borders in a chenille-type fabric. The panels are less textured, as it is difficult to keep a smooth appliqué outline on an uneven surface.

Size of pillow: 17¾ in. square
Size of each finished panel: 6 in. square
½ in. seam allowance throughout

■ Draft and make four Leaf and Berry blocks, varying the number of leaves and berries. Use the middle-size leaf template on page 65 for the leaves and a coin about 1 in. across as the template for the berries. Press from the back and trim panels to 6½ in. square. Sew the top and bottom panels together and press the seams in opposite directions. Then sew the two strips together and press the vertical seam either way.

■ Center the block on the muslin square, pin it in place, and quilt over the seams. The muslin square will protect the raw seam edges from fraying inside the pillow.

■ From the red chenille-type fabric, cut two 19 x 4-in. strips and two 12½ x 4-in. strips for the borders. With right sides together, stitch the short red border strips to the sides of the appliqué block (through the layer of muslin) and press the seams away from the block. Repeat with the top and bottom borders. Topstitch the red fabric around the appliqué block.

■ Cut two backing pieces measuring 19 x 10 in.. With right sides together, baste the two back pieces together along one long side, taking a ½-in. seam allowance. Machine stitch from each corner for 1½ in. Press the seam open and lay the zipper right side down on the wrong side of the seam. Baste and then machine stitch the zipper in place. Remove the basting.

■ Open the zipper. With right sides together, machine stitch all around the pillow cover, snip off the excess fabric on the corners, then turn the cover right side out. Topstitch around the edge of the pillow.

You will need

- 6-in. square of black cotton fabric for the leaves
- Scraps of red cotton fabric for the berries
- Two 8-in. squares each of two shades of cream
- 19½ in. red chenille-type fabric for the back and borders
- 19½-in. square of muslin or light cotton
- 16-in. zipper
- 18-in. square pillow form
- Matching thread

Butterfly and branch appliqué pillow

This pillow has a slightly textured furnishing-fabric backing with appliqué motifs in floral fabrics. Making it is a good way of using up lots of scrap-bag snippets or for recycling memory scraps from favorite clothes.

Size of pillow: 16½ in. square

½ in. seam allowance throughout

■ Using the Butterfly and middle-size Leaf templates on page 65 and 71, cut nine leaf shapes and a butterfly from a variety of fabrics. Cut a 19½-in. square of furnishing fabric for the pillow front. Draw a chalk curve diagonally across the front of the pillow and pin the leaves on either side of the line, with the butterfly top left.

■ Change the thread color for each motif. The backing fabric is opaque so all the threads can be drawn to the back and tied without the risk of show-through. First stitch the leaves, then satin stitch the branch to secure all the threads of the leaves. Finally, work the butterfly—the wings first and then the body.

■ Press from the back and trim to 17¼ in. square, then baste to the batting. Outline quilt ¼ in. away from the appliqué (see page 159) without breaking off, but working around the contours of the design.

You will need

- Scraps of cotton fabric for the appliqué
- 19½ in. slightly textured furnishing-weight fabric
- 17¾-in. square of 2-oz polyester batting
- 16-in. zipper
- 16-in. square pillow form
- Matching thread

■ Cut two 17¼ x 9-in. pieces of furnishing fabric for the back of the pillow. With right sides together, baste the back pieces together along a long edge, taking a ½-in. seam. Machine stitch from each corner for 1 in. Press the seam open and lay the zipper right side down on the wrong side of the seam. Baste and then machine stitch the zipper in place. Remove the basting.

■ With right sides together, stitch the pillow front to the back. Turn right side out and topstitch the edges.

Bird and leaf ring pillow

You could use fabric scraps from the curtains and bed covers to create this pretty vintage-style pillow.

Size of pillow: 21 in. square
Size of finished block: 11 in. square
½ in. seam allowance throughout

■ Referring to the Bird and Leaf Ring appliqué blocks (see pages 66–67), draft, cut, and appliqué the motifs to the background fabric. Trim to 12 in. square when stitched and pressed.

■ For the frames, cut one strip of each fabric across the full width, 1¾ in. deep—and then cut these into lengths 4–8 in. long and piece end to end in random order to make a long strip. Press the seams in the same direction along the length of the strip.

■ With right sides together, join the frame strip to the side edges, cutting off the excess as you proceed. Press flat, then add the top and bottom frame strips.

■ Repeat to make a second frame around the block.

You will need

- Scraps of small-patterned cottons for the appliqué leaves and bird wing, plus a 5-in. square of fabric for the bird
- 13-in. square of background fabric
- Three different strips of furnishing-weight fabrics for the frames, 2 in. wide
- 21½ in. cream-and-pink furnishing-weight fabric for the back and borders
- 21½-in. square of 2-oz batting
- 21½ x 1-in. strip of hook-and-loop tape
- 21-in. square pillow form
- Matching thread

■ Cut four border strips from the length of fabric, 3½ in. wide. Sew on the border strip, first to the side edges (trimming off the excess length), then to the top and bottom edges. Press the seams toward the border.

■ Baste the pillow top to the batting. Outline quilt the motif (see page 159), stitching about ¼ in. away. Quilt over the long frame seams and the border seams.

■ For the back, cut two pieces measuring 21½ x 12½ in. Fold over one long edge of one piece to the wrong side by ½ in. and press. Separate the two halves of the hook-and-loop tape and pin one half just below the fold to hide the raw edge of the fabric and stitch along each edge. On the other back piece, fold the fabric over to the right side and attach the remaining piece of hook-and-loop tape in the same way.

■ Stick the two back pieces together. Pin the patchwork right side down on the pillow back. Machine stitch all around, trim the edges, snip off any excess fabric on the corners, and turn the cover right side out. Topstitch around the edge of the pillow, matching the thread color to the fabric.

Fallen leaves pillow

The oak, maple, and ash leaves are arranged on the linen background to look like fallen leaves, with acorns and keys strewn among them.

Size of pillow: 23 in. square
Size of finished block: 15½ in. square
½ in. seam allowance throughout

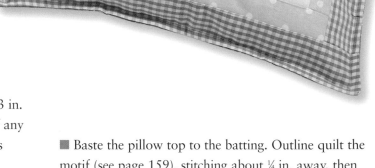

■ Referring to the Leaf motifs (see pages 70–71), draft, cut, and appliqué the motifs to the background fabric. The oak leaf is 6½ in. long, the maples 5½ and 3 in., and the ash leaves 4 in. long. Work the leaf vein detailing last and reduce the stitch width to 1 as you stitch. Press from the back and trim to 16 in. square.

■ With right sides together, sew the frame strips to the side edges of the block, cutting off any excess as you proceed. Press the seams away from the block, then add the top and bottom frame strips.

■ Cut four border strips from the length of fabric, 3 in. wide. Sew them first to the side edges (trimming off any excess), then to the top and bottom. Press the seams away from the block.

■ Baste the pillow top to the batting. Outline quilt the motif (see page 159), stitching about ¼ in. away, then quilt over the frame and border seams.

■ Cut two 24 x 12½-in. pieces for the back. With right sides together, baste the back pieces together along one long side taking a ½-in. seam allowance. Machine stitch from each corner for 2 in. Press the seam open and lay the zipper right side down on the wrong side of the seam. Baste and then machine stitch the zipper in place. Remove the basting.

■ Open the zipper. Pin the patchwork right side down on the pillow back. Machine stitch all around, snip off the excess fabric on the corners, and turn the cover right side out. Topstitch around the edge of the pillow.

You will need

- Scraps of cotton fabric for the appliqué
- 17¾-in. square of linen for the block background
- Four 20- x 2-in. strips of furnishing-weight fabric for the frame
- 24 in. furnishing-weight fabric for the back and borders
- 24-in. square of 2-oz polyester batting
- 20-in. zipper
- 23-in. square pillow form
- Matching thread

Hearts pillowcase

Heart shapes are often seen on old quilts and the timelessness of gingham gives a traditional rustic look. The border is folded back on itself to give more body and edged with a narrow strip of gingham that echoes the fabrics used in the appliqué. You could appliqué the same motif across the tops of sheets to create a matching set of bed linen. French seams give the pillowcase a neat finish.

Size of pillowcase: 19 x 24¾ in.
Size of border: 6¾ in. deep

■ With right sides together, stitch the binding strip across one short side of the linen, stitching ¾ in. from the edge. Fold the binding strip over to the other side of the piece, fold under ½ in. of the strip, and hand stitch it in place. Stitch and fold along the lines of the gingham to get a neat, crisp edge.

■ Referring to the Hearts motifs (see page 68), draft and appliqué the hearts along the short edge on which you machine stitched the binding.

■ Fold and hem stitch the other short side—so that the neat side is on the other side of the fabric from the appliqué.

■ Fold the appliquéd edge back to give a 6½-in. flap, with the appliqué showing. Now fold the case in half so that the fold line of the appliqué is level with the back edge. Stitch the side seams on the right side of the fabric, taking a ½-in. seam. Trim the seam to ¼ in. to neaten any stray threads, turn the pillowcase inside out and stitch the side seams again. Turn the pillowcase right side out.

You will need

● 20½- x 57-in. piece of strong white cotton or linen
● 2- x 2½-in. strip of gingham for the binding
● Scraps of cotton fabric for the appliqué
● Matching thread

Daisy and Checker patch bag

This simple square tote bag combines appliqué with a seven-patch Checker block. The patchwork is lined at the front and French seamed.

Size of bag: 17 in. square
Size of finished block: 12 in.

■ Referring to the Daisy motif (see page 67) and the Checkers block (see page 39), draft the block 13 in. square and cut the fabrics. Cut the gingham fabric used for the daisies diagonal to the grain, to contrast with the gingham used elsewhere on the block, which is cut on the straight of grain. Appliqué the daisies to the large checker squares.

■ Lay the patches out in sequence, placing the small squares randomly, and piece the block. Piece vertical strips 1, 4, and 7 first. Then piece the small squares in strips 2 and 3 into horizontal pairs and sew them to the large appliquéd squares; repeat for strips 5 and 6. Press the seams in alternate directions strip to strip. Finally, sew all the vertical strips together and press the seams in the same direction across the block.

■ Cut four 18½ x 3½-in. strips of gingham for the borders. Attach the borders to the top and bottom of the block, then trim off any excess. Then attach borders to the side edges. Press the seams away from the block.

You will need

- Scraps of cotton fabric for the appliqué
- Four 4-in. dark blue squares for Checker center squares
- 33 small squares in assorted blue and cream fabrics, each 2¼ in. square
- 18½ in. blue gingham for the borders, back, and handles
- 18½ in. square of light cotton lining
- Matching thread

■ With right sides together, stitch the lining square to the top edge of the front of the bag and press flat. Quilt along the border seams (see page 159) to hold the lining to the patchwork.

■ Cut a 18½-in. square of gingham for the back. With wrong sides together, stitch the front of the bag to the back along the sides and bottom. Trim the seam and turn the bag inside out. Stitch around the same three sides and turn right side out.

■ Cut two 15¾ x 2¼-in. strips of gingham for handles. With right sides together, fold in half lengthwise and machine stitch along the long unfolded edge. Turn right side out.

■ On both the front and back, on the inside of the bag, stitch the handle ends 4½ in. in from the sides, so that the handles hang down into the bag. Stitch in place, level with the border quilt line. Pull the handles up and stitch all around the top of the bag ½ in. from the top of the bag to secure the handles.

Bluebell bag

Light floral fabrics are appliquéd onto a background in furnishing-weight fabric on this bag.

Size of bag: 16 x 17¾ in. with a 3½-in. gusset
Length of handles: 22 in.
Size of finished block: 6¾ x 9 in.
½ in. seam allowance throughout

■ Referring to the Bluebell motifs (see page 72), draft and make one block and then trim the background fabric to 7½ x 10 in.

■ With right sides together, sew the blue strip to the top and bottom of the appliqué block, trimming off the excess, and press the seams away from the block. Then frame the sides and press the seams away from the block.

■ With right sides together, frame the top and bottom of the appliqué block with the pink fabric, trimming off the excess as you proceed, then frame the sides, each time pressing the seams away from the block. Lay the panel on the batting and baste it in place. Outline quilt the bluebell and then quilt along the seams (see page 159).

■ With right sides together, stitch the two pieces of lining fabric together around three sides, leaving a 6-in. gap in one seam.

■ From the pink spotted fabric, cut two 3 x 22½-in. strips across the width for the handles. Fold in half lengthwise, turn under the edges, and topstitch.

■ Cut a back piece measuring 17 x 19¼ in. and strips 4½ in. wide for the gusset, joined together to total 56 in. Right sides together, stitch the gusset strip around the sides and base of the bag front, and then do the same to sew on the back.

■ Pin the handles to the top of the bag 5 in. from the sides. With right sides together, pull the lining over the bag and stitch around the top.

■ Turn the bag right side out through the gap in the lining and hand stitch closed. Push the lining into the bag and topstitch to hold in place. Pinch the gusset seams together and topstitch all the way around, front and back.

You will need

- Scraps of cotton fabric for the appliqué
- 8½- x 12-in. piece of cream furnishing-weight fabric for the appliqué background
- 2½ in. blue furnishing-weight fabric for the frame
- Two 4-in. strips of pink furnishing-weight fabric for the front borders
- 24 in. pink spotted furnishing-weight fabric for the back, sides, and handles
- Two 20-in. squares of lining fabric
- 20-in. square of 2-oz polyester batting
- Matching thread

Daisy knitting bag

Perfect for holding all your yarn and knitting needles, this little bag has an appliqué daisy framed with printed lawns and a floral border. The pattern scale varies for contrast.

Size of bag: 16 x 20½ in.
Size of finished block: 6¼ in. square
½ in. seam allowance throughout

■ Referring to the Daisy motif (see page 73), draft and make one block, then trim the background fabric to 7 in. square.

■ Frame the top and bottom of the block with the cream fabric strip, trimming off the excess as you proceed, and then frame the sides. Repeat with the pink fabric, each time pressing the seams away from the block.

■ From the aqua floral furnishing-weight fabric, cut a 17 x 24-in. piece for the back of bag. From the remaining fabric, cut lengthwise two 3½ x 24-in. side borders; from the width of the fabric, cut a 3½ x 11½-in. strip for the bottom border and a 10¼ x 11½-in. strip for the top

border. Sew on the top and bottom borders, and then the side borders and press the seams away from the block.

■ Lay the bag on the batting and baste it in place. Outline quilt the daisy (see page 159) and then quilt along the seams.

■ Stitch the front of the bag to the back along the lower edge and then stitch the two lining pieces to each other along one short edge. With right sides together, stitch the lining to the bag along the top edges.

■ Stitch the side seams for the lining and the bag separately, leaving a 9½ in. gap at the top of each.

■ Pinch the bottom corners together so that the side and bottom seams are in line and stitch across about 1½ in. in from the corners.

■ Turn the bag right side out. Push the lining into the bag, fold in and stitch it to the bag along the gaps in the side seams.

■ Fold over the top of the bag to a depth of 3½ in. over the hoops, and hand stitch.

You will need

- *Scraps of cotton fabric for the appliqué*
- *8-in. square of cream fabric for the appliqué background*
- *2-in. strip of each of cream and pink floral fabrics for the frames, cut across the full width*
- *24 in. floral furnishing-weight fabric in aqua for the back and front borders*
- *17- x 24-in. piece of 2-oz polyester batting*
- *Two 17- x 24-in. pieces of lining fabric*
- *Ready-made plastic or cane hoop handles, 8 in. in diameter*
- *Matching thread*

Butterflies and Bees hanging

Rummage through your scrap bag for small-patterned fabrics in blues and greens—about 25 are used here. The hanging has an outline-quilted appliqué panel on a linen background and a patchwork border in printed lawns.

Size of hanging: 22 x 26 in.

¼ in. seam allowance throughout

■ Referring to the Butterfly and Bee motifs (see pages 65-67), draft and cut motifs. On the background fabric, draw branches in chalk or lightly in pencil. Pin pieces in place.

■ Changing the thread color for each motif, first stitch the leaves, drawing the start and finish threads to the back, and satin stitch the branches last. This will secure all the threads of the leaves. Work the butterfly wings first, then the body. Trim the threads at the back to avoid show-through. Press from the back and trim the background fabric to 16½ x 20½ in.

■ From scraps in random order, piece a border strip 3 in. wide x 104 in. long finished size and press all the

seams in the same direction. Sew the border strip to the top and bottom edges of the panel, cutting to length as you proceed. Press the seams away from the center. Now sew the border to the side edges and press.

■ Place the backing fabric right side down on your work surface, with the batting on top, and the appliqué block right side up on top of the batting. Baste the layers together; the batting and backing should be about 1 in. larger than the front.

■ Outline quilt the appliqué (see page 159), stitching about ¼ in. from the motifs. Quilt the patchwork border along the seams, either "in the ditch" or on the seams.

■ Trim off the excess backing and batting.

■ Bind the edges from the back (see page 172) and topstitch, padding it with scraps of batting.

You will need

- Colorful scraps of cotton fabric for the appliqué
- 18- x 22-in. piece of linen for the background
- About 40 4-in. squares or strips 4 in. wide and up to 4 in. long for the patchwork border
- 23½- x 27½-in. piece of lining fabric or calico for the backing
- 23½- x 27½-in. piece of 2-oz polyester batting
- 104- x 2-in. strip of fabric, or equivalent seamed, for the binding
- Matching thread

Bird and tulip ring quilt

This 16-block double-bed quilt uses the tulip, butterfly, and bees motifs, with some of the tulips arranged in bunches and some appliquéd onto satin-stitch rings. The appliqué blocks are framed with randomly pieced fabric strips and the same fabrics are used in the mitered stripe borders.

Size of quilt: 96 x 106 in.
Size of each finished block: 9 in. square
Width of border: 10½ in.
¼ in. seam allowance throughout

■ Referring to the appliqué blocks section, plan 16 different blocks and cut the templates and fabrics. Pin the motifs in place on the background fabric; remember that the background will be trimmed later, so keep the design within a 8-in. window. Satin stitch or work by hand and press from the back. Trim the blocks to 9¾ in. square.

■ Cut the fabrics for the frames into 3-in. strips across the width of the fabric, then cut these strips into lengths

5–8 in. long. Piece about half of them end to end at random. Press the seams in the same direction and stitch to the block edges, one side after another, trimming to length as you proceed. Press the seams away from the blocks.

■ Lay the blocks out in sequence and piece into four vertical strips. Press the seams in alternate directions from block to block. Sew the strips together. Press all the vertical seams in the same direction across the quilt.

■ Piece more frame strips together, press, and sew to the outer edges of the quilt top, framing it twice. Press the seams away from the center of the quilt.

■ Cut the fabric for the borders into 11-in. strips 2½–3½ in. wide. Piece all the border strips together long edge to long edge, at random, and press the seams in the same direction. Sew to the quilt top, mitering the corners (see page 171).

■ Piece the remainder of the frame strips and frame the entire quilt top again. Piece the remainder of the border strips to the top edge of the quilt only. Finally, frame the entire quilt again.

■ Lay the backing wrong side up with the batting on top. Lay the quilt top right side up on the batting and backing, and baste through all three layers vertically, horizontally, and diagonally (see page 157).

■ Machine or hand-quilt about ¼ in. from the block motifs, following the contours (see page 159). Now quilt the frames around the blocks, starting in the center of the quilt and working outward. My quilt lines are on the

You will need

- 10-in. squares of floral cotton fabrics in two fabrics each pink, blue, and green for the appliqué
- 16 12-in. squares of white cotton fabric for the block backgrounds
- 6 in. each of 26 floral cotton fabrics in different tones of pink, blue, cream, and green for the frames
- 11 in. each of 15 fabrics in predominantly pink and cream tones for the borders
- 21 in. pink floral cotton fabric for the binding
- 102- x 114-in. piece of white cotton fabric, or the equivalent seamed, for the backing
- 102- x 114-in. piece of 2-oz polyester batting
- Matching thread

long edges of the frame fabrics. Then quilt between the blocks. Finally, quilt the seams on the border and the outer frames. Remove the basting carefully—it may be caught by machine quilting stitches.

■ Trim away the excess batting and backing.

■ Cut the binding fabric into nine 2½-in. strips across the width of the fabric, sew together to make a continuous length, and press the seams. Fold over one long edge by about ½ in. and press. Bind from the back (see page 172), padding with strips of batting as you proceed.

Butterfly and tulip quilt

This 18-block quilt with appliqué borders uses the tulip, butterfly, and dragonfly motifs. Two patchwork corners in Diamond Squares add extra interest. The quilt is worked on a white cotton ground, with printed lawn appliqué, and machine quilted.

Size of quilt: 47 x 77 in.

Size of each finished block:

10 in. square

Width of border: 6 in.

¼ in. seam allowance throughout

■ First, cut the background fabric for the top and bottom borders from the width of white cotton fabric to 8½ x 33 in. and the side borders from the remaining length to 8½ x 70 in. Then cut 18 7-in. squares. (All these backing fabrics will be trimmed to size and shape once appliquéd and pressed.)

You will need

- 2½ yd white cotton for background
- 4 in. floral lawns, in six fabrics, two tones of green, cream sprig, and apricot for the appliqué and Diamond Squares corners
- 12 in. of fabric A for the block frames, 15 in. of fabrics B and C, and 28 in. fabric D for the block and outer frames
- 16 in. dark apricot lawn for the binding
- 55- x 85-in. piece of white cotton fabric or the equivalent seamed, for backing
- 55- x 85-in. piece of 2-oz polyester batting
- Matching thread

■ Referring to the appliqué block section (see pages 64–65), draft and appliqué 18 blocks with tulip and butterfly motifs. (The number of motifs and choice of fabric is random.) Press from the back and trim to 6½ in. square.

■ Cut frame strips across the width of the fabric, 2½ in. deep. From fabrics A and D cut four strips each; from fabrics B and C cut five strips each.

■ Frame the blocks—four each with fabrics A and D and five each with fabrics B and C—stitching the sides first and then the top and bottom. Press the seams away from the blocks.

■ Lay the blocks out in sequence and piece three vertical strips of six blocks each. Press the seams in alternate directions on each strip. Sew the strips together and press all the vertical seams in the same direction across the quilt.

■ Cut and pin motifs on the border strips. (You will need 12 tulips, about 16 leaves, six butterflies, and six dragonflies.) On the top and bottom borders draw in chalk or in pencil two tulip stems curving away from each other about 12 in. long, centered. Draw two pairs of stems on each of the side borders roughly 6 in. and 20 in. in from the left edges. Press the border strips and trim to 6½ x 68 in. and 6½ x 31½ in..

■ Referring to the Diamond squares border (see page 60), draft and make two 6-in. blocks. Sew one to the top of one side border and one to the bottom of the other border.

■ Sew the top and bottom borders to the quilt top and press the seams outward. Then sew on the side borders.

■ Cut six outer frame strips 2½ in. wide across the width of fabric D, sew together in one continuous strip, and press. Sew to the top and bottom of the quilt top, snipping off the excess, and then to the sides.

■ Lay the batting on the backing fabric and then center the quilt top on top. The backing and batting should be larger all around than the quilt top; the excess will be trimmed off once the piece has been quilted. Baste through all three layers vertically, horizontally, and diagonally (see page 157). Machine or hand-quilt about ¼ in. from the block motifs, following the contours (see page 159).

■ Now quilt the frames, starting in the center of the quilt and working outward. My quilt lines are on the very edge of each frame fabric. Then quilt between the blocks.

■ Finally quilt around the border motifs, the border edge, and the outer frame.

■ Remove the basting carefully—it may be caught by machine quilting stitches—and trim off the excess batting and backing.

■ Cut the binding fabric across the width of the fabric into six strips 2½ in. wide. Sew them together to make a continuous strip and press the seams. Fold over one long edge by about ½ in. and press. Bind from the back (see page 172), padding with strips of wadding as you go.

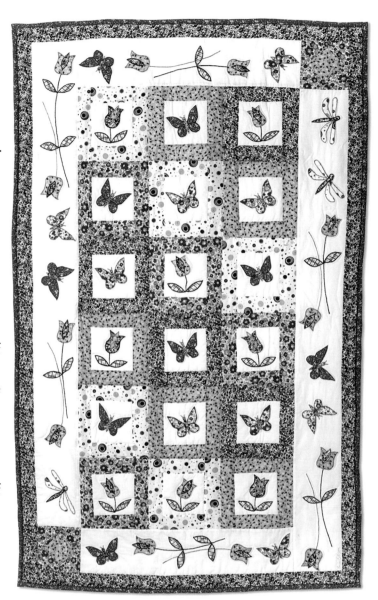

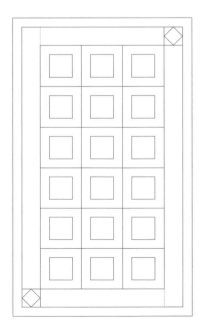

Orange Peel quilt

Hand appliquéd and quilted, this cover could be used as a crib quilt or as a throw across the width of a bed.

Size of quilt: 41 x 61 in.
Size of each finished block: 8¼ in.
Width of finished border: 6¼ in.
Width of finished sashing: 2 in.
¼ in. seam allowance throughout

■ Referring to the Orange Peel block (see page 88), draft and piece 15 identical blocks from the white and the yellow patterned fabrics—each with two patches with white lozenges on yellow and two with yellow on white.

■ From the length of the plain yellow fabric, cut two border strips 7½ in. wide for the side borders. From the remaining width, cut two border strips 7½ in. wide. Next, from the remaining length cut five strips 2¾ in. wide for the sashing and four strips 1½ in. wide for the binding.

■ Lay the blocks out in sequence. Piece them into three vertical strips of five blocks each, with sashing (cut from the length as required) in between, and press the seams toward the sashing. The sashing has intersection squares at each block corner. Cut ten 9-in. sashing lengths and eight 2¾-in. squares from the remaining sashing strip and join into two alternating strips long/square/ long/square

and so on. Press the seams away from the squares. Join the vertical block strips with intersecting square sashing between, and press the seams toward the sashing.

■ Add the top and bottom, and then the side, borders.

■ Lay the backing wrong side up and cover with the batting. Lay the quilt top right side up on the batting and backing, and baste well, in a vertical, horizontal, and diagonal grid (see page 157). Press seams away from the center of the quilt.

■ Quilt along the edge of the motifs and inside them, about ½ in. from the edge (see page 159). Quilt next to the sashing and then work the lozenges and rings. Use the appliqué template reduced to 3½ in. long for the lozenges. Finally, quilt the borders with ½-in. diagonal channels.

■ Fold over one long edge of each binding strip by about ½ in. and press. Bind from the front (see page 173), padding with strips of batting as you proceed.

You will need

● 1 yd each of white and patterned yellow fabric for patchwork
● 69 in. plain yellow fabric for sashing, borders, and binding
● 67 in. cotton fabric, 45 in. wide, or the equivalent seamed, for the backing
● 67- x 47-in. piece of 2-oz. polyester batting
● Matching thread

TECHNIQUES

This useful section provides all the tips and advice you will need when working by hand or machine—from choosing a fabric and cutting motifs or patches through to setting and preparing a quilt and finishing your work.

Fabrics

Any fabrics can be used in patchwork and appliqué, from light silks and cottons to heavy wools. However, bear in mind that some fabrics wear faster than others, some need dry cleaning, and some crease easily, which is problematic if quilted on to batting that cannot take a hot iron. The best advice is to choose compatible fabrics, and also avoid mixing weights.

■ Fabric labels often state they have been preshrunk and are colorfast. If you want to test, soak a sample in very warm soapy water. When cool, wring, and blot vigorously on white cotton to see if any dye transfers.

■ For quilts, 100 percent cotton is best since it lays flat for marking, cutting, and stitching, and holds a crease well. Cotton quality is measured by the number of threads to the inch. Choose either 78 square or 68 square— anything less is too loosely woven. "Square" means there are an equal number of warp and weft threads, so the pull on these "even weave" cottons is equal lengthwise and crosswise.

■ In polyester/cotton mixes, the thread count is uneven so the stretch is different, making it crease resistant. This uneven stretch can make the material pucker on seams and some poly cottons have a slight sheen (unlike most cottons), so mixing them with other fabrics can sometimes make a quilt look uneven.

■ Grain lines should be uniform across a quilt. To find the grain of a fabric, fold it, and hold and stretch by the selvages. If there are no ripples you have found the grain. If a fabric has been printed slightly off grain and the design is small or random, follow the true grain. If the pattern has an obvious repeat, then visually it is best to follow the design rather than the grain, but a big discrepancy will make piecing more difficult as the fabric will stretch.

Quilt preparation

Before your design can be quilted, it should be backed and padded. Back quilts with one of the fabrics used on the top, or seam pure cotton lengths to the desired width. Avoid poly cotton sheeting because it will stretch, gather, or pucker. The layer of padding that lies between the quilt top and the backing is called batting.

■ Synthetic batting is light, springy, easy to stitch, and washes well. It comes in different weights, known as lofts—2 oz, 4 oz, 6 oz, and upward— and in pale or dark colors.

■ Most modern cotton batting has been prepared to hold together well. It will have been bleached, preshrunk and had the seeds removed, so its texture is as uniform as that of a synthetic batting. To achieve the wrinkled look of an old quilt, choose a cotton batting that has been carded and bleached but not pre-shrunk. Wash the quilt when completed to shrink the batting inside the quilt.

■ Silk batting is costly but warm and easy to work. It needs close quilting to keep it in place.

■ Natural battings need to be quilted at intervals of ½–1¼ in. A cotton/synthetic mix can be quilted at 2–4 in. intervals, and synthetics will stay put with much larger unquilted areas. Batting fibers may eventually work their way through quilt tops and backings unless you use tight even-weave cottons for the top and backing.

■ The backing fabric and batting should extend at least 4 in. beyond the edges of a quilt top to allow for the shrinkage that occurs during quilting. If you need to join backing fabric, it is better to make two joins that fall roughly along each side of the bed rather than down the center.

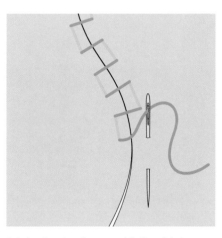

Joining batting for use with fine fabric

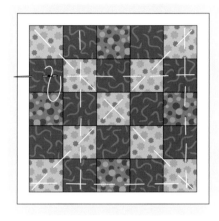

Basting a grid through all three layers

■ To join batting so that no ridge shows through, lay the two pieces edge to edge and ladder stitch them together. If the fabric is especially fine, overlap the two pieces by about 4 in. and cut a curved line along the length. Remove the excess, butt the two pieces together, and ladder stitch, using matching thread to avoid show-through. Stitch across the gap, down ½ in. and back to the other side. Keep the stitching loose or the batting may buckle.

■ Lay the backing fabric wrong side up on a flat surface and anchor it in place with tape or weights. Lay the batting over it, then place the quilt top on it, right side up. Baste a grid, about 12 in. square, and also a cross diagonally through the center. Use fine white basting thread and milliner's needles to make long stitches. You could also use large safety pins, evenly spaced about every 12 in., or a basting gun, which pierces the layers with plastic tabs. Long straight pins with glass heads are useful if you are working on a small area, but may come out when you are quilting a large area.

Quilting

Quilting can be done by hand or using a sewing machine. For hand quilting, use a large hoop or quilting frame because, although you can work without either of these, this risks layers becoming dislodged, even when they are well secured with basting. Machine quilting is much faster than hand quilting and, at its simplest, is just as unobtrusive a way of keeping the layers of a quilt together. It can also be highly decorative and intricate.

Hand quilting

For a traditional look, use white or cream thread throughout, even when quilting across dark fabrics. Alternatively, match the fabric color or use a contrasting thread. You can reflect any patchwork or appliqué design you are using by stitching along seams ("stitch in the ditch" quilting) or outlining motifs with stitched lines about ¼ in. apart ("echo" quilting). Otherwise, a diamond grid all over the quilt, diagonal or curved channels about 1¼ in. apart (see Orange Peel page 88), or complex plume, flower, chain, or rope designs can be used.

Rope design

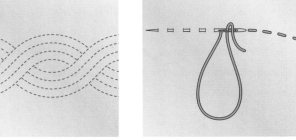

Four stitches at a time

■ To mark the design on the quilt top, use a quilter's pencil for a fine silvery line, chalk, or a pen that has "disappearing" ink. These marks will vanish either with time or water—check that the marks stay long enough for your purposes, and that they really do disappear, on a piece of spare fabric before drawing on the quilt top. Simple curves and straight lines can be scored on the fabric with a tapestry needle. For complex patterns, either make your own templates or buy plastic ones with pattern perforations. Work on small areas and mark only as much as you need each time.

■ If you are using a hoop, start in the center and work outward. If you have a full-sized quilt frame, start at one end of the quilt and work your way across it.

■ Use the smallest "sharps" needle you can manage for small and evenly spaced stitches. Quilting thread is a little sturdier than sewing thread. You can run ordinary thread though beeswax to toughen it. Use lengths of 18 in. at the most because the thread wears and frays at the needle's eye.

■ To start, pull the thread through the backing to the front, having tied a small knot in the end. Tug it a little so that the knot lodges in the batting—do the same to secure at the finish. If the quilting design is large or complex, use several needles, working as far as you can reach with each one before moving the work in the hoop or frame. The running stitches should be as tiny and even as possible—about six stitches to 1¼ in. If the batting is plump or the fabrics heavy, stab the needle straight down, pull the thread through, then stab stitch straight up. On lighter weight fabrics, rock the needle up and down, gathering about four stitches on the needle before pulling the thread through. A thimble on the finger underneath is essential to guide the needle point back to the quilt top.

Machine quilting

Prepare and baste your blocks carefully because the quilt top will be rolled and re-rolled, and squeezed through the sewing machine. Match the thread color to the quilt top, or if you want the stitching to be visible, use a slightly darker or paler thread—too much contrast and the line becomes very prominent. If you need to mark quilting lines, use a quilter's pencil, as for hand quilting.

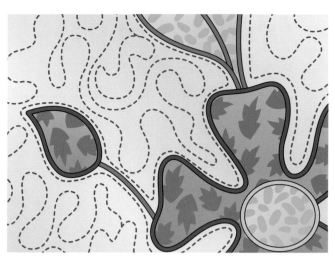

Vermicelli

■ Under the machine foot is a ridged area with sharp, pointed peaks. The foot presses the work toward these "feed dogs" and, as they rise and fall, they pull the work along while the needle stitches. This is a problem when quilting because the batting resists the pressure, so the lower layer of the "quilt sandwich" moves along faster than the top and puckers. Some machines have plates to cover the feed dogs, or they can be lowered, while some have variable pressure settings.

■ A "walking foot" locks into the feed dogs to hold the layers tight and keep them moving at the same speed. However, it is only really useful for stitching straight lines, not curves. A "free-embroidery foot" with the machine set on "darning" allows you to stitch in any direction. This foot generally has a small ring that the needle passes through, and the trunk of the foot is springy, so you can stitch through thick layers without downward pressure. You have to push and pull the work manually as you stitch—it will not move along otherwise. Place your hands flat on the work, either side of the needle. If working on very small areas, a 8 in. hoop will hold the work taut and flat and you can push the hoop without the danger of your hands getting too close to the needle. Be careful not to tug at the work because, if the needle is pulled, it may bend enough to miss the hole in the needle plate and snap.

■ Roll the quilt top from one side toward the center so it fits under the machine. Always start quilting in the middle of the work and move outward to the edges. To start, stitch a few reverse stitches. Do the same to finish or, for a neater look, draw the threads to the back and

thread through the fabric with a needle. You may need to slacken the tension of the top thread.

■ If the quilt has continuous lines, start at the top, work downward and then move to the right to continue. When you have reached the right-hand edge, re-roll the quilt, and work from bottom upward, again starting from the center. Work methodically, and never leave unquilted islands in heavily quilted areas because these isolated patches will puff up while the surrounding area becomes tightened with the quilting and will never lie flat.

■ If you have pressed the seams open, you can quilt right in the seam. Use a ballpoint needle so as not to split the seam stitches. The quilting will not show at all as the stitching will disappear between the joined fabrics. If the seams have been pressed to one side, you can "stitch in the ditch," right next to the seam. To give greater strength, stitch on the seam allowance.

■ On appliqué work it is essential to use an embroidery foot so you can maneuvre around shapes. Quilt either right next to the edge of the motif or outline it by stitching about ¼ in. away—called 'outline' quilting. "Vermicelli," or meandering, can be used to give texture to a background. First outline the motif, then stitch random curves and loops. As you are pushing and pulling the work yourself, you can even draw shapes or letters with the thread.

Patchwork techniques

Patchwork quilts can be put together in two main ways—with blocks or with "all-over," or mosaic, designs. The blocks, which comprise pieced squares of patchwork, are stitched together across a quilt top, either edge to edge, alternating with plain blocks or separated from each other with sashing strips (see page 170). All-over designs have one or more geometric shapes—hexagons, for instance—pieced together without any separation or sashing. Block patchwork can be worked by hand or machine, while all-over patchwork is traditionally worked by hand over papers.

Block patchwork

Blocks can be drafted in any size, although it can be difficult to work in sizes that are much smaller than those described in the block section. When your block is complete, it will be ½ in. larger than your paper draft because it will have a ¼ in. seam allowance along all four edges.

■ On graph paper, draw a square the size of the finished block. In the square, mark out the grid (four-patch, five-patch, or whatever you wish) and divide it into individual patches, marking the grain lines. These should run parallel with the sides of the block (fans and the eight-point star are exceptions), so when piecing two patches together, the grain matches – if it doesn't, the edge of one patch will stretch more than the edge of the other and the two won't fit together. Most blocks have repeating patches, so draft only the dark-colored section on the block diagrams, and make templates for each different size and direction shape—for example, Odd Fellow's Chain needs just one triangle and one square template whereas Old Maid's Puzzle needs two different-sized triangles and one square template.

■ Draw a sketch of the entire block with grain lines and fabric choices marked to keep as reference because it's very easy to get confused—if you put the work away for any length of time, it's easy to forget the piecing sequence entirely.

■ Cut out the graph paper templates and glue them to cardboard. Add a seam allowance of ¼ in. all around each shape and cut out the finished templates. Make sure there is a grain line on each template.

Cutting

Selvages stretch less than the body of the fabric because the thread count is double, so always trim them off. Cutting accurately is important—a minor discrepancy will multiply itself across a quilt.

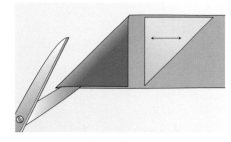

Grain along a short side

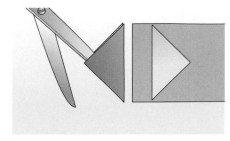

Grain along the long edge

■ Draw around the templates lightly in pencil on the wrong side of the fabric and scissor cut just a couple of thicknesses at a time. You can cut through several layers at a time with a rotary cutter. A nonslip design board is useful for keeping cut pieces in sequence. A piece of cardboard 4 in. larger than the block and covered with cotton batting, felt, or terry cloth is ideal.

■ There is a quick way to cut several same-size triangles from the same fabric. For triangles with the grain along a short side, use the template to cut strips the width of a short side, fold the strip diagonally and cut along the fold. For those with the grain running along the long edge, cut strips the width of the long side, fold the strip diagonally into quarters and cut along the fold lines. Check the block instructions to see if shapes need to be identical or mirror image—"quick cut" triangles will be mirror image. The method is not suitable if the fabric has a directional pattern or noticeable weave direction, or is striped.

Quick-cut triangles

Piecing and pressing

Use thread matching the darker fabric and take a ¼ in. seam allowance.

■ **Hand piecing** Secure the start and finish with a few overstitches —knots can come undone or show through as bumps. Work about five running stitches then a backstitch before another set of running stitches. The backstitches stop the running stitches from gathering, and also, should the thread break, keep the seam secure.

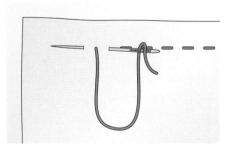

Running stitch

■ **Machine piecing** Patches can be joined one at a time using reverse stitching at the start and finish, but it is much faster to "chain piece" and just as secure if you use a very small stitch (15 to the inch). Piece two pieces together and stitch right on to the next pair and so on. Snip the thread between the chain-pieced patches to separate them.

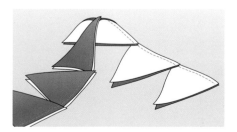

Chain-pieced patches

■ Press the seams on each block as you proceed, toward the darkest fabric, away from central squares. When piecing patches together, alternate up and down on the horizontal seams, so on one strip they lie one way and on the next strip they lie the other way. Then press vertical seams in the same direction across the block and across the quilt top. It is sometimes impossible to follow all the rules but the aim is to avoid bulk at the seams and, whenever possible, to avoid show-through of dark colors. If there is show-through, trim away the dark fabric on the seams and on the corners.

■ If you are going to hand quilt, avoiding bulk is even more important and it may be best to open seams out. This puts more strain on the seams but it will be compensated for by the quilting.

■ While you work, gently run your finger along a fold before joining to the next piece. Fabric stretches more along the bias than along the grain, so be very careful when pressing diagonals not to pull and distort the pieces. If you decide to iron each patch as you go, use pressure rather than push. Set a crease using steam and let the fabric cool before moving it because it can stretch when hot. Ironing through a layer of cloth on to a well-padded board will minimize the risk of the seam layers imprinting onto the right side of the work. Iron well once the block is finished, and again press rather than push.

■ When piecing two strips together, pin either side of the horizontal seams with the pin heads outward, so they are easy to remove as you stitch toward them. The seams will sit well together, one slotting into the dip of the other, as long as the horizontal seams are pressed in different directions. If they don't fit exactly, tug them a little so they do. If you have pressed the seams open, put a pin right through the horizontal seams to keep them level.

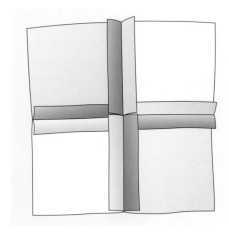

Pressing seams open

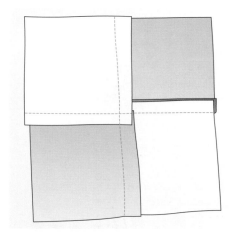

Pressing seams in alternate directions

Piecing strips

Assembling a block

Some blocks, such as Ohio Star, are pieced in equal-width, vertical strips while others are pieced in square (Bear Paw) or triangular (Lady of the Lake) units before assembly. Follow the directions given for each block.

■ Place the patches in sequence on a nonslip board. Piece and press the smallest shapes first.

■ Piece these patches into strips, pressing seams in alternate directions.

■ Piece the vertical strips, pinning either side of the cross seams to keep the intersection true. Press the seams in the same direction across the block.

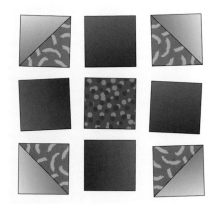

Assemble the patches in sequence

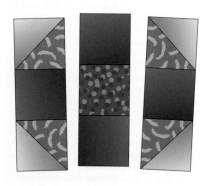

Sewing together in strips

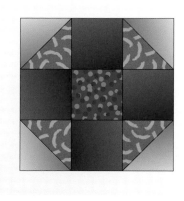

Block assembled

Foundation blocks

These are generally worked from the center outward, with strips pieced one by one around the edges of a central square onto a backing fabric. Log Cabin is a good example, but for a more random use of odd-shaped snippets of fabric, Crazy Patchwork is hard to beat.

Crazy patchwork

Size of finished block: 13 in. square

■ The first piece pinned to the backing and worked around on this block was the four-sided dark turquoise shape in the center. This was framed with strips, and then further strips were added at odd angles. It is sometimes easiest to piece a couple of snippets together and stitch these in place. Always work from the center of the block outward. Press and trim to shape.

Blocks with curves

These may look daunting but are not difficult. Make templates for a square with a cut-out curve and for a quarter circle, adding a seam allowance of ¼ in. along every edge. The cut-out curve in the square will appear too small for the quarter circle curve due to the seam allowance. If there are several curves on a block, you will need to make several templates in the relevant sizes. Always work the smallest first.

■ Fold each square and quarter circle in half and crease mid curve as a matching guide. Place a quarter circle on a square, right sides together, and pin where the creases match on the curve. Fold over and pull the straight edges at each the end of the curve so that they are level. Turn the work over, because it is easier to stitch the stretchy concave curve to the quarter-circle curve, and pin with the pin heads outward so you can remove them easily as you proceed.

■ As you stitch, tug gently at the top fabric to keep the fabric edges level and make the curves fit. Press, gently ironing the quarter circle flat. If necessary, nudge the curve into shape with the tip of the iron from the front.

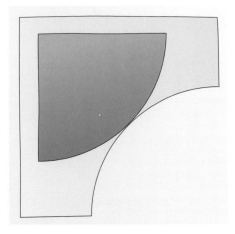

Match the creases on the curves

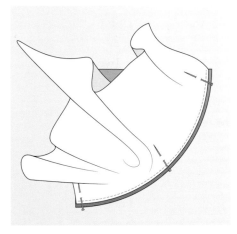

Pin before you stitch

All-over designs

The technique for sewing geometrical shapes together into a mosaic pattern is called paper piecing. Each patch is folded over a paper template and then the patches are stitched together edge to edge. The method is slow and painstaking, both in preparation and stitching time, but any all-over mosaic design can be worked in this way, and the shapes can vary from squares and triangles to diamonds, octagons, and hexagons, as in this example.

■ Draft the template (see page 160). Cut an equal number of lightweight paper hexagons (without seam allowance added), enough to make up the finished quilt, and the same number of fabric pieces, adding a ¼ in. turning allowance. Two edges should be aligned on the straight grain. Pin the papers to the back of the patches, fold the edges over and baste. The securing knot should be on the right side to make it easier to remove.

■ Place two hexagons right sides together and whipstitch along one edge, right on the fold line. The stitches should be tiny, the thread matching the darker fabric. Place a third hexagon face to face on one of the joined hexagons and stitch from the center out. Pinch together to bring the next edges level and stitch. Any tenting will disappear once the rosette is complete.

■ Sew the rosettes together to make the entire quilt top, press flat, then remove the basting—the papers will come away easily.

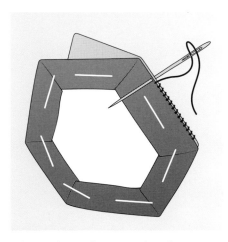

Whipstitch two shapes together along one straight side

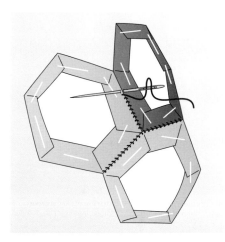

Sew on a third shape, starting at the center

Continue piecing shapes until the rosette is complete

Appliqué

Appliqué is the stitching of one fabric to another. Snippets of expensive cloth can go a long way when sewn to a less expensive background fabric. The background should be the same weight or heavier than the appliqué to avoid the fabric tearing or the stitching wearing.

Hand appliqué

The grain line should run along the line of symmetry of a motif, to give equal stretch around it. Match the grain of the motif to that of the background fabric if the motif is large, so that if the finished work is stretched, the motif will stretch as much as the background and there won't be any extra strain put on the stitching or fabrics. If the motifs are tiny, discrepancy of stretch will be minimal.

■ Trace or enlarge a motif on paper and mark the grain line. Cut out, adding a ¼ in. turning allowance along every edge. Stick the paper shape to thin cardboard (or place on sandpaper, which won't slip). On the wrong side of the motif fabric, draw around the template lightly, using a pencil, chalk, or a quilter's pen, and then cut out the motif.

■ Fold the turning allowance to the back and baste, making sure the securing knot is on the right side of the fabric, so the thread is easy to remove later. Snip into acute angles. On points, first fold the point in, then fold the two sides inward.

■ For really crisp edges, cut another paper template without the seam allowance and pin it to the wrong side of the fabric motif (which has the allowance). Fold the turning allowance over the paper template and baste the edges. Press on the wrong side and remove the basting and paper.

■ Pin or baste the motif, or layers of motifs, to the background fabric. On intricate shapes, such as Hawaiian appliqué, pin or baste the motif firmly to the background—not around the edges of the shape but through the middle. Fold the turning allowance in with the point of the needle as you stitch, snipping into angles as you reach them.

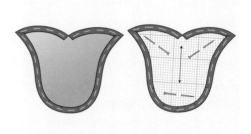

Use a paper template for a crisp edge

Pinning and basting

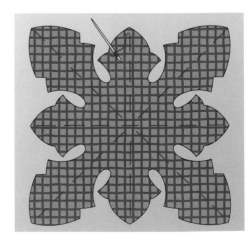

Basting Hawaiian appliqué

Stitching

If motifs overlap, stitch the one closest to the background fabric first, starting and finishing under an overlap for neatness. Secure with overstitching rather than a knot, which could make a bump or come undone. Slipstitch hardly shows but if the piece is going to have a lot of wear—children's clothes, for example—Paris stitch is far more secure. You can pad motifs with a little batting as you proceed.

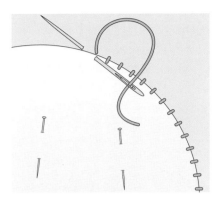

Slipstitch

■ **Slipstitch** should be worked in small, regular stitches—close to invisible. Match the thread to the darkest color in the appliqué fabric and use the smallest 'sharps' needle you can work with—short with a tiny eye. Start stitching on a straight or smooth part of the motif, not a point or corner, and work counterclockwise with the motif toward you. Pick up ⅛ in. of motif fabric along the fold, insert the needle into the background fabric and pick up ⅛ in. parallel to the edge of the motif. Make extra stitches on points to secure well and finish with a few overstitches.

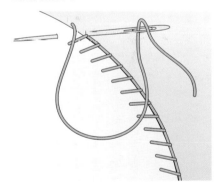

Paris stitch 1

■ **Paris stitch** is very strong. Although worked over the motif and not along the turning-allowance fold, if the stitches are kept small and regularly spaced and arc in thread matching the appliqué, they should not be too noticeable. Working counterclockwise with the motif toward you, bring the needle through to the front of the motif, ⅛ in. from its edge. Insert the needle into the backing ⅛ in. diagonally right, and travel the needle horizontally left to reappear above the motif. Backstitch and travel diagonally down and left to reappear through the motif, ⅛ in. from its edge.

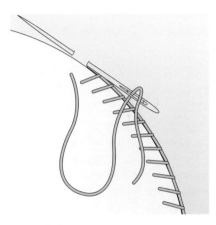

Paris stitch 2

■ **Blanket stitch** is a decorative stitch worked in contrasting color thread. Embroidery floss is a good choice. Use crewel needles, which have long eyes. Working counterclockwise, with the motif away from you, bring the needle through the background fabric just next to the motif. Insert the needle through the motif, diagonally up and right, and up to ¼ in. away. Travel the needle vertically down and through the background, just next to the motif, looping the thread around the needle as shown.

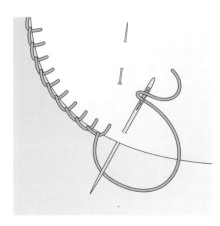

Blanket stitch

■ **Detail running stitching** is quick to work. Gather about four running stitches on a needle before pulling the thread through.

■ **Stem stitch** gives a solid stitched line. Working from left to right, insert the needle from the front to the back ¼ in. right. Travel the needle left and reappear ⅛ in. right of where you first started. Repeat, always keeping the thread below the line of stitching.

■ **Chain stitch** is very decorative and about ⅛ in. wide. Working from right to left, take a ¼ in. stitch and loop the thread around the needle before pulling through. Reinsert the needle in the same hole and take another ¼ in. stitch.

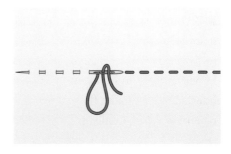

Running stitch

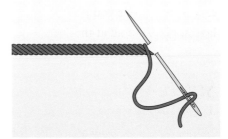

Stem stitch

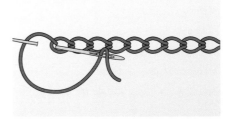

Chain stitch

The grapes here are detailed with stem stitch

Machine appliqué

Just as with hand appliqué, the grain of the motif and background should match if the motif is large. Both hand and machine appliqué can distort the background fabric, so always cut the background about 10 percent larger than required and trim to size once stitched and pressed. Press finished work from the back on a padded surface.

■ Make the template as for hand appliqué but without the turning allowance—the satin stitch will cover the edge of the fabric and stop it from fraying.

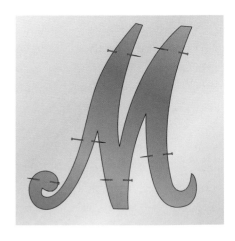

Pinning motif to the background

■ If you want to use loose-weave or stretchy fabrics, or material that frays easily, iron fusible web or interfacing to the back of the fabric before cutting out the motif. However, bear in mind that even the lightest weight interfacing can make flimsy material look flat and a little papery and, eventually, the glues will discolor the fabric.

■ Pin or baste the motif on to the background fabric, with the pins across the line of stitching to make them easy to remove as you proceed. If the design has several layers, pin them all at the start.

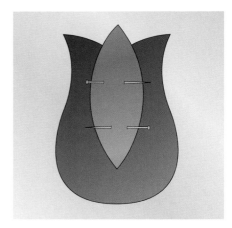

Pinning two layers to the background

Stitching

As the satin stitch is visible and outlines the motif, choose thread in colors either matching or slightly darker than the fabric—on patterned fabric you could vary the thread color from one motif to another.

Use the same brand and weight of thread for the top of the machine and the bobbin. If your machine doesn't auto-select thread tension, you may need to loosen the tension of the top thread a little to stop the bobbin thread from being pulled to the front. If the background fabric is pale or see through, use a pale bobbin thread. Otherwise match it to the top color.

■ Set the machine to a close satin stitch, width 3 or 4, and stitch clockwise around the motif, right along the edge. The motif will be to the left of the needle. Start on an inside curve or point, lay the top thread along the line to be stitched and stitch over it for about 1¼ in. to conceal and secure it, then trim it close.

■ Turn the work gently as you stitch to maneuver around curves. When you reach a point or deep curve, keep the needle in the fabric, lift the presser foot, and turn the work around the needle. Lower the foot and continue.

■ At the end, draw the threads to the back, tie them together and trim the ends close. If there is a risk of show-through, draw the threads to the back and, using a needle, pass them through the satin-stitch channel. Then trim the ends close.

■ If the design has overlapping motifs, stitch the one closest to the background fabric first, starting and finishing just under an overlap. If there is no risk of show-through, draw the threads to the front, trim, and tuck them under the next layer.

■ On a design such as leaves on a satin-stitch stem, stitch the leaves first, then the stem. Just covering the leaf tips will keep the top threads secure and the bobbin threads can be trimmed later. You could draw the leaf threads to the front and conceal them under the stem.

■ Narrow the stitch width to make points. Always add detail last, once the motif has been stitched in place, and, again, narrow the stitch width.

Satin stitch is used here for the leaves and stem

Sashing and borders

Blocks can be joined edge to edge or alternated with plain ones, or sashing—strips of another fabric—can be inserted between them. Adding differently patterned squares at junctions can add interest to a simple design. Press seams toward the sashing.

■ **Plain sashing** Join blocks together in vertical strips, using sashing between each block. Then stitch a length of sashing to one vertical edge and piece a second vertical block strip to it. The four-patch sampler quilt on page 116 is a good example.

■ **Intersecting squares** Cut sashing strips the same lengths as the blocks, and make some small squares, equal in width to the sashing strips but in differently patterned fabric. Join blocks together in vertical strips,

using sashing between each block. Piece sashing strips to the squares to make a long strip, and stitch this to one vertical edge of a strip of blocks. Then piece a second vertical strip of blocks to the sashing strip.

■ **Tiny squares** As a variation, sashing strips can be made of tiny squares, as in Counting Fish, or of a border design, such as Sawtooth or Flying Geese. Make lengths of sashing from squares, or based on a border strip, and join as for plain sashing.

Borders

Frame a quilt top or hanging by giving it a border before binding. The border can be a patchwork or appliqué strip, or simply a narrow length of material around the quilt top in the same, or contrasting, fabric as the sashing. Cut the border fabric into strips across the fabric width, and make one long strip by stitching them together, end to end, and pressing the seams all in the same direction. Cut lengths as needed.

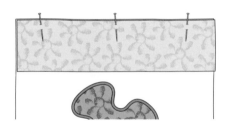

Pin the border strip to the work

Lapped border

■ Cut two border strips the same length as the quilt top. With right sides together, pin the strips to two opposite edges of the work and stitch them ¼ in. from the edge. Flap back the strips and press flat. Cut two more border strips that measure the length of the remaining sides of the quilt plus the attached border strips. Pin, stitch, and flap back as before, and press flat.

■ Using contrasting fabric on the corners, like intersecting squares on sashing, adds interest. To do this, stitch border

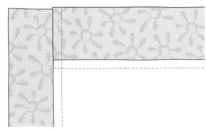

Cut the side strips the length of the sides plus the borders

strips along top and bottom edges and press, as before. Cut two more border strips the length of the sides and add squares at each end, so that the whole of each strip is equal in length to the work plus the already attached borders. Then piece these strips to the two remaining edges.

Mitered corners

■ These are difficult to make but give a neat appearance to a quilt top, like a picture frame. Cut a border strip for the top edge, so that it extends by a length equal to its width at both ends. Do this for all four sides. Then, right sides together, pin the first strip to the top of the quilt, top edges aligning. Fold the strip ends down at a 45° angle and cut along the fold.

■ Stitch the border strip to the quilt top, starting and stopping ¼ in. from each end and flap back so that the right side is now uppermost. Then pin a border strip to the side of the quilt. This should reach the top edge of the top strip.

■ Stitch this in place, starting and stopping ¼ in. (6 mm) from the end of the quilt so as not to stitch over the already attached border. Fold the strip end down at a 45° angle and cut along the fold.

■ Do not flap back the side border but align the diagonals, right sides together—which will entail folding in the top strip—pin, and stitch from the quilt to the outside corner.

■ Flap back, press open the seam, and press the borders flat.

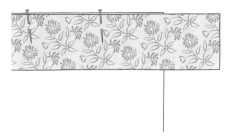

Mitered corners 1

Mitered corners 2

Mitered corners 3

Mitered corners 4

Mitered corners 5

Binding a quilt

Binding strips can be cut on the straight grain of the fabric or on the bias. They can be stitched to the back of the work, folded over, and machine topstitched on the front, or stitched to the front of the work, folded over, and hand stitched on the back. Bias strips allow you to bind around the corners of a quilt because they stretch; otherwise you need to bind one edge at a time. Alternatively, you can "self bind" either by folding the backing fabric to the front and topstitching, or folding the quilt top to the back of the quilt and hand stitching in place.

Binding from the back

■ Cut the fabric for the binding into straight-cut strips about 2½ in. wide and join into one length. Fold under and press ½ in. along one long edge.

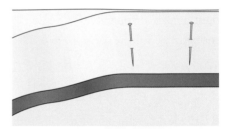

Binding from the back 1

■ Pin the raw edge of the right side of the binding to the back of the quilt and then stitch ½ in. from the edge. Snip off the excess binding. Fold the other (folded) edge of the binding over to the front of the quilt, pin, and topstitch, adding a little of the batting remnants as you proceed.

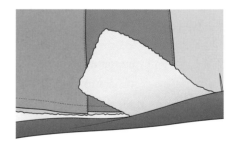

Binding from the back 2

■ Working clockwise around the quilt, pin and stitch the next length of binding in place, leaving about ½ in. extra at the start to be folded in and secured by hand later. On the last side, leave extra at both the start and the finish for turnings.

Binding from the front

■ With right sides together, pin and stitch the raw edge of the straight-cut binding along one side of the quilt. Snip off the excess binding. Fold the folded edge of the binding over to the back of the quilt, pin, and hem, adding batting strips if desired.

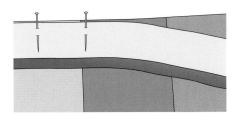

Binding from the front 1

■ Working clockwise around the quilt, pin and stitch the next length of binding, leaving about ½ in. extra at the start to be folded in and secured by hand later, when you hand stitch the back. On the last side, leave extra at both the start and the finish for turnings.

■ **Bias-cut binding** If you are using bias-cut binding strips, cut the strips diagonally across the fabric and sew them together along their diagonal edges—the strips will be at right angles as you stitch. Make a continuous strip long enough to bind the entire quilt.

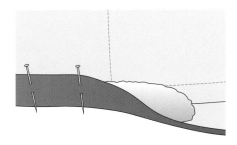

Binding from the front 2

Self binding

■ Trim the backing fabric of the quilt to within 2 in. of the quilt top, and the batting to about 1 in. of the quilt top. Position the layers (see below), then fold the backing fabric to the front of the quilt on opposite edges, folding under by ½ in. Hem by hand or machine topstitch. Fold over and stitch the remaining two edges as before, and hand stitch the corners to neaten. To self bind from the front, fold the quilt top over to the back of the work and hand stitch.

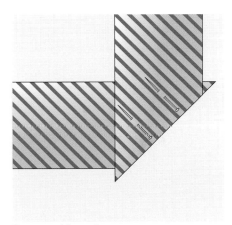

Seams on bias strips

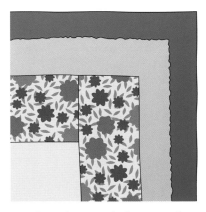

Lay the quilt top on the batting and backing

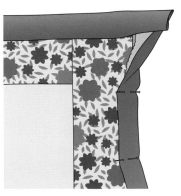

Fold the backing and batting to the front, pin, and stitch

Stitch corners by hand

Suppliers

Blackberry Patchworks Ltd.
408 N. Main Street
Piqua
Ohio 45356
Tel: 937-615-0877
Web: www.blackberrypatchworks.com

Clover Needlecraft Inc
1007 East Dominguez Street,
Suite K
Carson
California 90746
Tel: 310-516-7846

Colonial Needle, Inc.
74 Westmoreland Avenue
White Plains
New York 10606
Tel: 1-800-963-3353 (toll-free) or 914-946-7474 (local)
Fax: 914-946-7002
Web: www.colonialneedle.com

EZ Quilting by Wrights
85 South Street
West Warren
MA 01092
Tel: 800-628-9362
Web: www.ezquilt.com

Fons & Porter
54 Court
Winterset
Iowa
Tel: 1-888-985-1020
Web: www.fonsandporter.com

Gathering Fabric Quilt Shop
14450 Woodinville
Redmond Road
Woodinville
Washington 98072
Tel: 425-402-9034
Fax: 425-402-9134
Web: www.gatheringfabric.com

Heritage Quilt & Needlework
10939 N. 56th Street
Tampa
Florida 33617
Tel: 813-989-3993
Web: www.heritagequiltshop.com

Hingeley Road Quilt Shop
11284 Hwy 2
Floodwood
Minnesota 55736
218-476-3139
Web: www.hingeleyroadquiltshop.com

Hopscotch Quilt Shop
1401 20th Avenue
Coaldale, AB.
Canada T1M 1A2
Tel: 403-345-3910
Web: www.hopscotchquiltshop.com

Jeri's Quilt Patch
703 Brown-US2
Norway
Michigan 49870
Tel: 906-563-9620
Web: www.jerisquiltpatch.com

Life's A Stitch
516 Queen St. East
Sault Ste. Marie
Ontario P6A 2A1
Tel: 705-254-3339 (local) or 866-570-2062 (toll-free)
Web: www.lifesastitch.ca

Linda's Sew 'n So
216 W. Fayette Street
Celina
Ohio 45822
Tel: 419-586-2324
Web: www.sewnso.com

Patchworks
122 Main Street
Sayville
New York, 11782
Tel: 800-647-5596 (toll-free) or 631-589-4187 (local)
Web: www.patchworks.com

QuiltBug Quilt Shop
169 Main St, PO Box 273
Esperance
New York 12066
Tel: 888-817-6577 or 518-875-9400
Fax: 518-875-9401
Web: www.quiltbus.com

The Quilt Emporium
4918 Topanga Canyon Boulevard
Woodland Hills
California 91364
Tel/Fax: 818-704-8238
Web: www.quiltemporium.com

The Quilted Kitty
2295 So. 48th Street
Lincoln
Nebraska 68506
Tel 866-422-9292 (toll-free) or 402-420-9292 (local)
Web: www.quiltedkitty.com

Quilters' Paradise
713 8th Street
Baldwin City
Kansas 66006-0646
Tel: 1-888-256-9981 (toll-free) or 785-594-3477 (local)
Web: www.quiltingfabricsupply.com

Qwiltz Quilt Shop
112A West College Street
Bowdon
Georgia 30108
Tel: 770-258-3201 (local) or 1-866-479-4589 (toll-free)
Web: www.quiltsuppliesonline.com

Stacey's Quilty Conscience
5385 Peachtree Dunwoody Road
Suite 310
Atlanta
Georgia 30342
Web: www.quiltyconscience.com

Suzanne's Quilt Shop
9 First Street S.E.
Moultrie
Georgia 31768
Tel: 229-616-1013 (local) or 1-888-798-0934 (toll-free)
Fax: 229-616-1014
Web: www.suzannesquilts.com

Woodstock Quilt Supply
79 Tinker Street
Woodstock
New York 12498
Tel 845-679-0733
Web: www.quiltstock.com

Index